THE GIFT-GIVER'S COOKBOOK

by

Jane Green and
Judith Choate

SIMON AND SCHUSTER · NEW YORK

PUBLISHED BY SIMON AND SCHUSTER
ROCKEFELLER CENTER, 630 FIFTH AVENUE
NEW YORK, NEW YORK 10020

MANUFACTURED IN THE UNITED STATES OF AMERICA

To Matthew, Simon, Mickey, Chris and

Those other two who made it all possible

Contents

Introduction

WE THINK that there is nothing nicer to give or receive than a gift made in someone's kitchen, and we feel that most of our friends would agree. Particularly now that gift giving has become such a frenzied and commercialized activity, homemade gifts are unmistakably personal and convey to your friends, and also to your husband's business associates, that you have really given of yourself.

Throughout the year—and especially at Christmastime, while others are struggling with long shopping lists in overcrowded stores—you can remain in the warmth and friendliness of your own kitchen preparing gifts to please each recipient.

A well-stocked pantry or freezer of homemade goodies provides gifts for any occasion. Whenever we go to a party we present our hostess with something homemade: it can be a jar of jam or jelly, a fruit syrup or something as simple as salted or spiced nuts or an herbed rice. Whatever we choose is always welcomed! A bouquet of inexpensive kitchen gadgets and nonperishable homemade edibles is perfect for a housewarming or a wedding shower. Dime-store plastic toys packed with cookies or candy are great gifts for children. In fact, when any occasion calls for a gift, make it yourself!

We have found that it is not only a pleasure to receive homemade foods but even more delightful to make them. Working with a friend increases the fun, the yield, the recipes and provides a shoulder to cry on when the occasional kitchen disaster occurs. Your family can join in too: children love to make and decorate cutout cookies, and husbands can always be counted on to taste.

Homemade gifts cost very little. Our preparations start in midsummer when local fruits are ripe. Trips to the country yield wild berries and vegetables. In early August, peach orchards offer all you can pick, with immense savings over supermarket prices. And what a lovely way to spend the day! In early fall we all look forward to picking in the apple orchards. We have even enlisted friends and relatives across the country to send us their local nonperishable products—pecans from a Southern aunt, walnuts and dates from a brother in Southern California and fresh herbs from a friend's garden.

All through the year we save jars from instant coffee, baby food, mustard, mayonnaise, pickles, etc. They are the perfect sizes to hold homemade jams and jellies and eliminate the need to purchase jars made especially for this purpose. Coffee, nut, shortening and cookie tins, with your added decoration, make beautiful, personalized and cost-free containers for any confections. Fruit baskets (small ones like those in which Concord grapes, berries and cherry tomatoes are sold) also make marvelous gift containers when covered with aluminum foil or gift wrap and ribbon-tied.

In September, when the last batch of applesauce has been stored, we begin our Christmas baking with a fruitcake weekend. The first cakes are made from the recipes Judie's grandmother carried with her from Scotland in the early 1900's. She made her cakes in January and let them ripen all year long. Batches of light and dark fruitcakes are seasoned with brandy, wrapped and stored in a cool place, to make their first appearance on the Thanksgiving table along with the last one from the previous Christmas. Later on, we usually try a new recipe—a fruitcake richer, nuttier or more interesting than our usual one.

Recollections of Christmases past are filled with memories of holiday foods—the year the fruitcakes were especially good, the time our cookie-decorated tree was taken over by a colony of ants, the Gingerbread House whose roof kept shifting, the school-bus driver who started reminding us in June to be sure to remember his Christmas Date Bread, the Christmas Bubble Bread that kept rising until it pushed the oven door ajar. And all of them, even the disasters, are filled with smells and tastes that make holidays truly memorable.

The recipes contained in this book are those we feel can be most easily made ahead of time, in fairly large quantities, stored or frozen and shipped without damage. Helpful information in each of these areas is included in the book. And always *label* your homemade gifts; people like to know what they are eating. We once received a thank-you from the recipient of a huge basket of homemade gifts that said, "We had no idea what we were eating, but it was all delicious." Since then, we have labeled each container of a homemade food.

There is almost no limit to the variety of gifts that you and your kitchen can produce. Not only the recipes in this book, but favorite casseroles, soups or salads that can be transported in plastic containers make wonderful gifts. We are sharing with you the rewards of many hours in our kitchens. We feel it is the nicest way of saying, "We're friends."

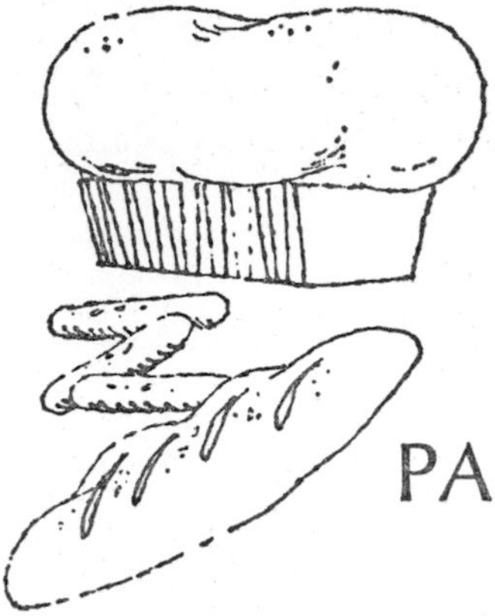

PART ONE

FROM THE OVEN

1 · Fruitcakes...and Others

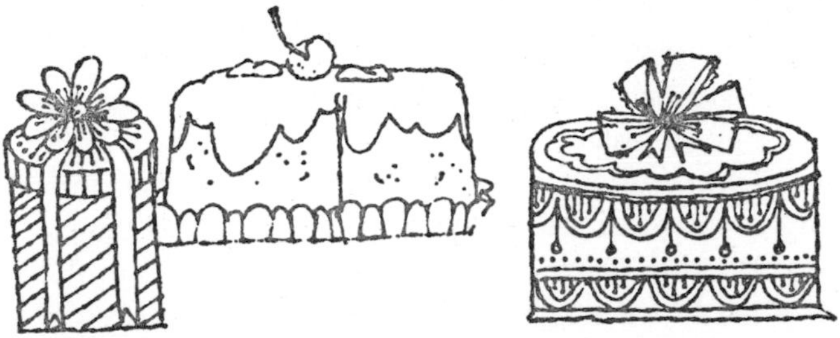

FRUITCAKES are most often seen on the Christmas table, but since they store well in a cool place and can be made in large quantities, they make excellent gifts all year round. All of the cakes listed under OTHERS may be prepared in advance and frozen.

Fruitcakes taste best and are least expensive when the chopped fruit is purchased in bulk. If you don't have a store specializing in dried fruits in your locale and you want to produce especially delicious cakes, we suggest that you order the fruits from one of the stores in our Shopping Guide (page 192). You can, of course, buy chopped fruit in jars, but the end result will be both costlier and drier. On the other hand, we suggest that you use spices freshly ground, as their flavor seems to hold up better through a long storage period.

Most of the recipes list the necessary equipment. It is important to use the same measuring utensils for each ingredient, as there is often a difference in sets of measuring cups and spoons. Also, a rubber spatula and wire cooling racks will make cake baking easier. If you follow the instructions as given, you should have no trouble presenting your family or friends with a delicious and attractive cake.

Almost all cake directions begin with "Cream butter and sugar until light and fluffy." This is one of the most important steps in successful cake making. Starting with the butter at room temperature, these two ingredients will be properly creamed when the sugar has lost its graininess and the color is quite pale. If they are improperly creamed, the result will be a tough cake.

A small pan of water placed on the bottom of the oven during the baking time will also produce a moister cake.

There are two methods of preparing pans for baking and for the storing of fruitcakes. You may line the pans either with greased heavy brown paper or with aluminum foil. If you use brown paper, you must remove it before wrapping the cake in a brandy-soaked cheesecloth for storage. If you use aluminum foil, it can be left on the cake as a storage wrapping. With the latter method, generously sprinkle brandy on the cake–individual taste will determine the amount. Either method requires airtight storage. An excellent container is a large plastic bag (like those sold as garbage-can liners) sealed tightly.

AGING: Fruitcakes can of course be eaten immediately, but everyone knows that conventional fruitcakes improve with aging. What this means is periodically unsealing the airtight wrapping, sprinkling the cakes with brandy and resealing them. This can be done every two or three weeks, depending on how strong a brandy flavor you want.

Note that fruitcakes are not generally frozen, since they keep for long periods without it.

When freezing other cakes, wrap them carefully in freezer wrap, label them and mark the date of baking. It is best not to freeze a cake for longer than three months. If you wish to frost or glaze the cake, this can be done either before or after freezing. Thaw a frozen cake at least one hour at room temperature before serving.

Plastic wrap, foil and disposable aluminum pans and paper goods make packaging and transporting gift cakes relatively simple.

There are endless ways to wrap and transport a loaf cake. For instance, loaf cakes may be wrapped airtight in aluminum foil and gift-wrapped, or the foil may be decorated with stick-on bows, ribbons or colored tape. Two or three loaf cakes can be placed in a shoe box or any other suitably sized box, which can be covered with adhesive-backed decorative paper or with gift wrap. Loaf cakes wrapped in clear plastic wrap and given in a ribbon-trimmed clear-plastic storage container are an attractive and useful gift.

Tube, layer or square cakes present a bit more difficulty. One of the easiest and prettiest methods of packaging is to cut a heavy piece of cardboard somewhat larger than your cake, cover it with foil and place the cake on it. Put cake and cardboard base on a large piece of cellophane or plastic wrap, which can then be pulled together at the top of the cake and tied with ribbon. You may also use a paper plate as a base, if you have one big enough to fit the cake. Cakes are generally so attractive that clear plastic wrap is all that is necessary to wrap them in. There are so many sizes of disposable aluminum pans that you may wish to bake and give your cake in one of them.

For a more festive and important gift, you can always accompany the cake with a fancy cake knife, a covered cake plate, dessert plates or perhaps even an antique cake plate. You can purchase inexpensive plastic cake plates in a cut-glass design at most variety stores—this is not costly, but does add to your gift. And don't forget to label the cake, so that the recipient will know what he is eating.

Fruitcakes

GRAMMA'S PLAIN LIGHT FRUITCAKE

Preheat oven to: 300 *degrees*
Utensils needed: 3 *8-inch loaf pans, foil-lined*
Baking time: 2 *to* 2½ *hours*

1 *cup unsalted butter*
1½ *cups sugar*
⅔ *cup white corn syrup*
4 *egg yolks*
1 *teaspoon soda*
1 *cup sour milk*
1½ *pounds currants*
1 *pound pitted dates*
1 *pound dark seedless raisins*
2 *cups chopped walnuts*
4½ *cups sifted flour*
2 *tablespoons freshly ground cinnamon*
4 *egg whites, stiffly beaten*

Cream the butter and sugar until light-yellow and fluffy. Add the syrup and egg yolks and beat well. Add the soda to the sour milk, stir well and pour into the creamed mixture. Stir in all fruits and nuts.

Sift one half of the flour, together with the cinnamon, into the creamed mixture. Mix with your hands and continue adding flour until you have achieved a soft batter.

Stiffly beat the egg whites and fold into the batter. Pour batter into prepared pans and bake at 300 degrees for approximately 2 hours, or until edges pull away from sides of pan.

Remove from pans and cool on wire racks. If stored over one month, moisten from time to time with brandy.

GRAMMA'S WHITE FRUITCAKE

Preheat oven to: 300 *degrees*
Utensils needed: 3 *8-inch loaf pans, foil-lined*
Baking time: 2 *to* 2½ *hours*

1 *cup unsalted butter*
1 *cup sugar*
1 *teaspoon almond extract*
1 *cup sliced blanched almonds*
1 *cup chopped citron*
1 *pound white seedless raisins*

1 *tablespoon grated lemon rind*	3 *cups sifted flour*
1 *pound chopped glazed fruit*	1 *teaspoon baking powder*
1 *cup candied green cherries*	8 *egg whites, stiffly beaten*

Cream the butter and sugar until pale and fluffy. Stir in almond extract. Dredge the nuts, citron, raisins, lemon rind, glazed fruit and cherries with ½ cup flour and add to the creamed mixture, mixing well.

Sift the remaining 2½ cups flour. Add 1 teaspoon baking powder to 1½ cups sifted flour and resift over the fruit mixture. Using hands, mix well. Add enough extra flour to make a soft, sticky batter. Stiffly beat the egg whites and fold them into the batter. Pour into prepared pans and bake at 300 degrees for about 2½ hours, or until edges pull away from the pan.

Remove cakes from pans, and cool on wire racks.

GRAMMA'S DARK FRUITCAKE

Preheat oven to: 300 *degrees*
Utensils needed: 10 6-*inch loaf pans, foil-lined*
Baking time: 2 *hours*

1½ *cups soft butter*	1 *pound white seedless raisins*
1½ *cups sugar*	1 *pound dark seedless raisins*
8 *egg yolks*	2 *pounds chopped glazed fruit*
⅔ *cup white corn syrup*	1½ *pounds whole pitted dates*
1 *teaspoon baking soda*	½ *pound green glazed cherries*
1 *cup sour milk*	½ *pound red glazed cherries*
½ *cup brandy (or fruit juice)*	½ *pound chopped citron*
1 *teaspoon orange extract*	¼ *pound chopped glazed pineapple*
2 *tablespoons freshly ground cinnamon or* 3 *tablespoons canned ground cinnamon*	*flour to make soft batter, about* 7 *cups*
1½ *cups sifted flour*	8 *egg whites*
1½ *cups chopped walnuts*	¼ *teaspoon cream of tartar*
1½ *pounds currants*	

Cream the butter and sugar until light-yellow and fluffy. Add egg yolks and corn syrup and beat well. Stir one teaspoon of baking soda into the sour milk and add to the creamed mixture. Continue mixing while you add the brandy, orange extract and cinnamon. Set aside.

In another bowl, place the nuts and fruits. Dredge them well with 1½ cups flour. Add the dredged fruits and nuts to the creamed mixture along with enough flour to make a soft batter. This must be mixed with your hands so that it will be easy to tell when a soft batter has been achieved. You will probably use about 7 cups of flour.

Add the cream of tartar to the egg whites in the large bowl of an electric mixer. Beat until stiff. Using your hands, lightly fold the stiff egg whites into the batter. Spoon batter into prepared pans, filling each about two-thirds full. Place a container of water in the bottom of the oven to prevent cakes from drying out.

Bake about 2 hours at 300 degrees, or until edges pull away from the sides of the pans. Remove from pans and cool on wire racks.

DARK FRUITCAKE

Preheat oven to: 350 *degrees*
Utensils needed: 5 1*-pound coffee cans, foil-lined*
Baking time: 45 *minutes to* 1 *hour*

3 *eggs, beaten lightly*
1 *cup sugar*
¾ *cup vegetable oil*
⅛ *cup brandy*
2 *cups mincemeat*
1 *cup chopped glazed fruit*
½ *cup chopped glazed orange peel*
½ *cup chopped dates*
½ *cup chopped prunes*
1 *cup chopped walnuts*
½ *cup chopped almonds*
4¾ *cups sifted flour*
½ *teaspoon salt*
1½ *teaspoons baking soda*
¼ *cup boiling water*

Combine the eggs, sugar, oil and brandy and beat for 2 minutes. Add all fruits and nuts to the egg mixture and mix well.

Sift the flour and salt together twice. Add to the fruit mixture and blend well. Add the baking soda to the boiling water and fold into the batter.

Pour the batter into prepared cans. Bake at 350 degrees for about 45 minutes, or until edges pull away from sides of cans. Remove from cans and cool on wire rack.

CANDLELIGHT DARK FRUITCAKE

Preheat oven to: 250 *degrees*
Utensils needed: 1 10-*inch tube pan, bottom lined with waxed paper*
Baking time: 4½ *hours*

1½ *cups pitted dried prunes*
1 *cup dried apricots*
2 *cups seedless raisins*
1 *cup yellow raisins*
1 *cup diced candied pineapple*
½ *cup sliced candied cherries*
1½ *cups diced candied orange peel*
1 *cup diced lemon peel*
1 *cup diced citron*
1 *cup chopped almonds*
1 *cup chopped pecans*
2½ *cups sifted flour*
2 *teaspoons baking powder*
1½ *teaspoons salt*
1 *tablespoon cinnamon*
1 *teaspoon allspice*
½ *teaspoon ground cloves*
1¼ *cups shortening*
1½ *cups sugar*
6 *eggs*
½ *cup pineapple or other juice*

Cut prunes and apricots into slices. Mix all the fruits with the nuts and 1 cup flour. Set aside.

Sift together the remaining flour, baking powder, salt and spices.

In another bowl, cream the shortening. Add sugar and beat until light and fluffy. Add eggs one at a time, beating well after each addition.

Add sifted dry ingredients alternately with the fruit juice to the shortening-sugar mixture. Pour batter over the fruit-nut mixture and mix well.

Pour mixture into prepared pan and place in oven, along with a shallow pan of water. Bake at 250 degrees for 4½ hours or until edges pull away from sides of pan. Let cake sit for 10 minutes in the oven, after the heat has been turned off, before removing from pan. Continue cooling on wire rack.

SOUTHERN DARK FRUITCAKE

Preheat oven to: 250 *degrees*
Utensils needed: 3 *9-inch tube pans, greased and floured*
Baking time: 2¼ *to* 3 *hours*

4 *cups sifted flour*
1 *pound soft butter*
2¼ *cups sugar*
1 *cup dark molasses*
12 *eggs, well beaten*
2 *teaspoons baking powder*
1 *cup milk*
1 *tablespoon cinnamon*
1 *tablespoon allspice*
1½ *teaspoons grated nutmeg*
½ *cup sherry*
½ *cup brandy*
2 *15-ounce packages raisins*
1 *package currants* (11 *ounces*)
½ *pound dried figs*
½ *pound citron, chopped*
½ *pound candied pineapple, chopped*
½ *pound diced mixed fruit*
2 *pounds chopped almonds*

Dredge fruits and nuts with 1 cup flour and set aside.

Cream butter and sugar together until light and fluffy. Beat in the molasses and then the well-beaten eggs. Add the remaining flour and the baking powder dissolved in the milk. Mix thoroughly. Add the spices mixed with the sherry and brandy. Add the dredged fruits and nuts.

Pour batter into prepared pans. Bake at 250 degrees for 2¼ to 3 hours, or until edges pull away from sides of pan. Cool thoroughly before removing from pans. Continue cooling on wire racks.

LIGHT YULE CAKE

Preheat oven to: 300 *degrees*
Utensils needed: 1 *9-inch loaf pan, greased and floured*
Baking time: 1¾ *hours*

1½ *cups whole Brazil nuts*
1½ *cups walnut pieces*
⅔ *cup chopped candied orange peel*
1 *pound whole pitted dates*
½ *cup red maraschino cherries*
½ *cup green maraschino cherries*

1 cup seedless white raisins
¾ cup sifted all-purpose flour
½ teaspoon baking powder
½ teaspoon salt
¾ cup sugar
3 eggs, beaten
1 teaspoon vanilla extract

Place nuts, dates, orange peel, cherries and raisins in a large bowl. Sift the flour, baking powder, salt and sugar together over the nuts and fruits. Mix well. Add beaten eggs to the fruit-nut-flour mixture. Continue mixing and add vanilla. Mix well.

Spoon mixture into prepared pan and bake in preheated 300-degree oven for about 1¾ hours, or until edges pull away from sides of pan. Cool cake in pan for 10 minutes. Loosen cake around edges and remove from pan to continue cooling on a wire rack.

VIRGINIA'S LIGHT FRUITCAKE

Preheat oven to: 300 *degrees*
Utensils needed: 5 *4-inch loaf pans, greased and floured*
Baking time: 1½ *hours*

1 cup butter
1 cup sugar
2 cups sifted flour
5 eggs, separated
2 tablespoons orange liqueur
1½ pounds candied apricots
½ pound candied pineapple
1 pound candied cherries
1 pound chopped walnuts
1 pound chopped pecans

Cream butter and sugar together until light and fluffy. Add flour, then egg yolks. Add the orange liqueur, then the fruits and nuts. Beat egg whites until light, and fold, as carefully as possible, into batter.

Pour into the prepared loaf pans. Bake at 300 degrees for 1½ hours or until edges pull away from sides of pans. Let cool in pans 10 minutes and remove to wire rack to cool.

LIGHT RADIANT LOAF

This is one of the easiest of fruitcakes. Unlike the others, it should be eaten promptly—or it may be frozen.

Preheat oven to: 325 *degrees*
Utensils needed: 1 *9-inch loaf pan, greased and floured*
Baking time: 1 *hour*

1 *egg, beaten*
¾ *cup milk*
½ *cup sugar*
3 *cups Bisquick*
½ *cup chopped walnuts*
1 *cup chopped glazed fruit*

To the beaten egg, add the milk and sugar. Stir well. Stirring continuously, sift the Bisquick into the egg mixture. Mix well. Add the chopped nuts and chopped glazed fruit. With a heavy spoon, or your hands, mix well.

Spoon mixture into prepared pan and bake at 325 degrees for 1 hour or until edges pull away from sides of pan. Remove from pan and cool on wire rack.

REBECCA'S EASY DARK FRUITCAKE

Preheat oven to: 325 *degrees*
Utensils needed: 1 *8-inch tube pan, greased and floured*
Baking time: 1¾ *to* 2 *hours*

1 *1-pound-4-ounce can of fruit cocktail, drained*
3 *teaspoons baking soda*
1 *teaspoon salt*
1 *teaspoon cinnamon*
3 *eggs*
2 *cups sugar*
3 *cups sifted flour*
1½ *cups chopped walnuts*
1½ *cups black raisins*
2 *ounces cognac or brandy*

Mix all ingredients in a large bowl and pour into prepared pan. Bake at 325 degrees for 1¾ to 2 hours, or until edges pull away from sides of pan. Cool in pan for 10 minutes, then remove to wire rack and finish cooling.

NO-BAKE FRUITCAKE

Quantity: 2 *cakes*

2 *cups chopped dates*
2 *cups dark seedless raisins*
1 *cup currants*
1 *cup chopped glazed fruit*
1 *cup chopped glazed pineapple*
½ *cup red glazed cherries*
½ *cup green glazed cherries*
2 *cups chopped almonds*
1 *cup chopped walnuts*
3 *cups miniature marshmallows*
4 *cups graham-cracker crumbs*
1 *teaspoon salt*
1 *teaspoon ground nutmeg*
1 *teaspoon ground cloves*
1 *teaspoon allspice*
1 *teaspoon cinnamon*
1 *can sweetened condensed milk*

Place the fruits, nuts and marshmallows in a large mixing bowl. Mix together well. Stir in the graham-cracker crumbs and the salt and spices. This should be done with your hands. Add the condensed milk and knead well. Divide the mixture in half, and roll each half into a loaf. Wrap each loaf tightly in foil or clear plastic wrap, and store in the refrigerator *at least* 24 hours before serving. It keeps well in a plastic refrigerator dish with a lid.

NOTE: When this fruitcake is given as a gift, the recipient should be told to refrigerate it immediately.

Other Cakes

BUNDT CAKE

Preheat oven to: 350 *degrees*
Utensils needed: 3-*quart bundt pan, greased and floured*
Baking time: 30 *to* 40 *minutes*

1 *cup butter*
2 *cups sugar*
3 *cups sifted flour*
4 *eggs*
1 *cup milk*
1 *teaspoon vanilla*
2 *teaspoons baking powder*
¼ *teaspoon salt*

Cream together the butter and sugar until light and fluffy. Add the flour a little bit at a time with one egg and ¼ cup milk. Beat well. Continue adding flour and eggs and milk until all are beaten in. Blend in the vanilla, baking powder and salt. Mix well.

Pour into prepared pan. Bake at 350 degrees for 30 to 40 minutes, or until edges pull away from sides of pan. Remove from pan and cool on wire rack.

Variations:
1. Mix in one cup finely chopped nuts.
2. Marbleize cake by loosely stirring in ¼ cup cocoa.

APRICOT-BRANDY POUND CAKE

Preheat oven to: 325 *degrees*
Utensils needed: 3-*quart bundt pan, greased and floured*
Baking time: 1¼ *hours*

1 *cup softened butter*
2½ *cups sugar*
6 *eggs*
1½ *teaspoons vanilla*
1½ *teaspoons orange extract*
3 *cups sifted* cake *flour*
¼ *teaspoon baking soda*
½ *teaspoon salt*
1 *cup sour cream*
½ *cup apricot brandy*

Cream butter and sugar together until light and fluffy. Add eggs one at a time, beating well after each addition. Add vanilla and orange extracts.

Sift together flour, baking soda and salt. Add alternately to butter-sugar mixture with the sour cream and brandy. Mix well.

Pour batter into prepared pan and bake at 325 degrees for 1¼ hours or until edges pull away from sides of pan. Cool in pan before removing cake. Continue cooling on wire rack.

JANE'S WALNUT POUND CAKE

Preheat oven to: 325 *degrees*
Utensils needed: 3 *9-inch loaf pans, lined with waxed paper, buttered* or *floured*
Baking time: 1 *hour*

1 *pound butter*
2 *cups sugar*
10 *eggs*
4 *cups sifted* cake *flour*
2 *cups finely chopped walnuts*
1 *tablespoon vanilla*

Cream butter thoroughly. Add sugar gradually, creaming with butter until mixture is very light and fluffy. Add eggs one at a time, beating well after each addition. Gradually stir in flour, blending until smooth. Stir in walnuts and vanilla and mix well. Pour into 3 prepared 9-inch loaf pans.

Bake at 325 degrees for 1 hour or until cake is springy to touch and toothpick inserted in the middle comes out clean. Remove from pan and cool on wire rack.

Variations: 1. For 1 of the 2 cups of finely chopped walnuts, substitute 1 cup chocolate bits.

2. Add to the basic mixture 1 teaspoon cinnamon and 2 teaspoons grated orange peel.

BLANCHE'S ORANGE POUND CAKE

Preheat oven to: 350 *degrees*
Utensils needed: 1 10*-inch tube pan, greased and floured*
Baking time: 40 *to* 50 *minutes*

¾ *cup butter*
1½ *cups sugar*
2 *eggs*
1 *teaspoon vanilla*
2 *cups sifted flour*
1 *teaspoon baking soda*
½ *teaspoon salt*
1 *cup sour cream*
1½ *teaspoons orange rind*

TOPPING
½ *cup sugar*
½ *cup orange juice*
4 *tablespoons orange liqueur (optional)*

Cream the butter and sugar together until light and fluffy. Add the eggs one at a time, beating well after each addition. Add the vanilla.

Sift together the flour, baking soda and salt. Gradually add the sifted dry ingredients to the butter-sugar mixture alternately with the sour cream. Beat well. Add the orange rind and mix well.

Pour into prepared pan. Bake at 350 degrees for 40 to 50 minutes, or until edges pull away from sides of pan. Remove cake from oven.

Boil together sugar and orange juice for topping. Add orange liqueur if desired. While cake is still hot, pour this mixture over the top. When cake is cold, remove from pan.

DELMONICO NUT CAKE

Preheat oven to: 350 *degrees* (325 *degrees for glass pan*)
Utensils needed: 1 9×13*-inch pan, greased and floured* or 3 8*-inch layer pans, greased and floured*
Baking time: 1 *hour* (9″ × 13″) *or* 25 *minutes* (*layers*)

½ *cup softened butter*
½ *cup vegetable shortening*
2 *cups sugar*
5 *egg yolks*

1 teaspoon vanilla
2 cups sifted flour
1 teaspoon baking soda
1 cup buttermilk
1 cup shredded coconut
1 cup chopped pecans
5 egg whites, stiffly beaten

Cream the butter and shortening thoroughly. Gradually add sugar; beat until light and fluffy. Add egg yolks and vanilla. Continue mixing.

Mix sifted flour with soda and sift together three times. Add to batter alternately with buttermilk, beginning and ending with dry ingredients. Stir in coconut and chopped pecans. Stir a heaping tablespoon of stiffly beaten egg white into the batter and beat vigorously by hand until blended. Carefully fold into batter the remaining egg whites.

Pour into prepared pans. Bake at 350 degrees (325 degrees for glass pans) for 1 hour for loaf pan or 25 minutes for layer pans or until edges pull away from sides of pan. Remove from pan and cool on wire rack. When cool, frost with Delmonico Cake Icing.

DELMONICO CAKE ICING

Utensils needed: Electric mixer with small bowl

8-ounce package cream cheese, softened
4 tablespoons softened butter
approximately ¾ box confectioner's sugar
1 teaspoon vanilla
⅓ cup finely chopped pecans

Beat the cream cheese and butter together until very smooth. Gradually add sugar; beat to spreading consistency. Blend in vanilla.

Cover sides and top of cake (and between layers for layer cake) with frosting. Sprinkle finely chopped pecans over top.

JUDIE'S RICH CHOCOLATE-CHIP CAKE

Preheat oven to: 350 *degrees*
Utensils needed: 1 *9-inch spring-form tube pan, greased and floured*
Baking time: Approximately 45 *minutes*

1 *cup condensed milk*
2 *squares unsweetened chocolate*
½ *cup butter*
1½ *cups sugar*
2 *eggs*
1 *teaspoon baking soda*
1 *cup milk*
2½ *cups sifted flour*
1 *teaspoon vanilla*
1 12-*ounce package chocolate bits*

Place condensed milk and chocolate squares in heavy saucepan over medium heat. Bring to boil; stir until mixture reaches pudding consistency. Remove from heat. Cool.

Cream butter and sugar until light and fluffy. Add eggs and beat into mixture. When well blended, add chocolate mixture. Stir the baking soda into the milk. Add to batter. Sift the flour into the batter and mix well. Stir in the vanilla. Fold in the chocolate bits, making sure that they are evenly distributed through the batter.

Pour into prepared pan. Bake at 350 degrees for about 45 minutes, or until edges pull away from sides of pan. Cool slightly in pan. Remove and finish cooling on wire rack. Serve at room temperature.

CALIFORNIA DATE CAKE

Preheat oven to: 350 *degrees*
Utensils needed: 1 8-*inch square cake pan, greased and floured*
Baking time: Approximately 40 *minutes*

1 *cup chopped dates*
1 *cup boiling water*
½ *cup softened butter*
1 *cup sugar*
1 *egg*
1⅔ *cups sifted flour*
¼ *teaspoon salt*
1 *teaspoon baking soda*
1 *cup chopped walnuts*

Cover the dates with the boiling water and set aside to cool.

In another bowl cream the butter, sugar and egg until light and smooth. Place the sifted flour, salt and soda in a sifter. Add the flour alternately with the cooled date mixture to the creamed ingredients. Mix well. Stir in the chopped nuts and blend well.

Bake in the prepared pan at 350 degrees for approximately 40 minutes, or until edges pull away from sides of pan. Cool in pan on wire rack. When cool, dust the top of the cake with powdered sugar. (If you are going to freeze the cake, do not dust top with sugar until ready for use.)

DATE CAKE

Preheat oven to: 350 *degrees*
Utensils needed: 1 *9-inch loaf pan, greased and floured*
Baking time: 45 *minutes*

1 *pound chopped walnuts*
1 *pound pitted dates*
1 *cup seedless raisins*
4 *egg yolks, slightly beaten*
1 *cup sugar*
1 *cup sifted flour*
2 *teaspoons baking powder*
1 *teaspoon vanilla*
4 *egg whites, stiffly beaten*

Place the walnuts, dates and raisins in a medium mixing bowl. Pour the beaten egg yolks over them and mix well. Add the sugar and stir until sugar starts to dissolve a bit.

Sift the flour and the baking powder into the mixture. Stir until flour is fully incorporated. Mix in the vanilla. Fold the stiffly beaten egg whites into the batter. Pour into prepared pan and bake at 350 degrees for 45 minutes or until edges pull away from sides of pan. Remove from pan and cool on wire rack.

BLACKBERRY-JAM SPICE CAKE

Preheat oven to: 325 *degrees*
Utensils needed: 1 10-*inch tube pan, greased and floured*
Baking time: 2 *to* 2½ *hours*

1 *cup softened sweet butter*
2 *cups sugar*
3 *eggs*
3 *cups sifted flour*
1 *teaspoon baking soda*
1 *cup buttermilk*
½ *teaspoon ground cloves*
½ *teaspoon nutmeg*
½ *teaspoon cinnamon*
½ *teaspoon ginger*
1 *cup seedless raisins*
1 *cup blackberry jam*
1 *cup chopped walnuts or pecans*
1 *cup diced glazed fruit*

Cream the butter and sugar. Add the eggs and beat until very light. Sift the flour with the soda and add to the butter mixture alternately with the buttermilk and spices until well mixed. Stir in the raisins, jam, nuts and glazed fruit. Mix well.

Pour batter into prepared pan and bake at 325 degrees for 2 to 2½ hours, or until edges pull away from sides of pan. Remove from pan at once and cool on wire rack.

RAISIN SPICE CAKE

Preheat oven to: 375 *degrees*
Utensils needed: 1 9-*inch loaf pan, greased and floured*
Baking time: ½ *hour at* 375 *degrees plus* 1 *hour at* 350 *degrees*

1 *pound seedless raisins*
water to cover
½ *cup unsalted butter*
1½ *cups sugar*
2 *eggs*
2 *cups sifted flour*
1 *teaspoon baking soda*
1 *teaspoon nutmeg*
2 *teaspoons cinnamon*
½ *teaspoon salt*
1 *cup chopped walnuts*

Cover the raisins with water; boil 20 minutes. Drain and reserve 1 cup liquid. Set aside. Cream the butter and sugar until light and fluffy. Add the eggs, blending well. Sift all dry ingredients alternately with the raisin liquid into the creamed mixture. Stir together. Fold in the raisins and chopped nuts.

Pour into prepared pan. Bake ½ hour at 375 degrees. Turn heat down to 350 degrees and continue baking for 1 hour or until edges pull away from sides of pan. Remove from pan and cool on wire rack.

HONEY SPICE CAKE

Preheat oven to: 350 *degrees*
Utensils needed: 1 *8-inch-square loaf pan, greased and floured*
Baking time: About 45 *minutes*

½ *cup butter*
1 *cup sugar*
½ *teaspoon salt*
1 *egg*
2 *cups sifted flour*
1 *teaspoon baking soda*
½ *teaspoon ground cloves*
½ *teaspoon ground mace*
1½ *teaspoons cinnamon*
1 *cup sour milk*
⅓ *cup chopped nuts*

TOPPING
2 *tablespoons softened butter*
4 *tablespoons honey*
2 *tablespoons heavy cream*
1 *cup chopped nuts*

Cream the butter and sugar until light and fluffy. Add the salt and egg and blend well. Place the sifted flour, soda and spices in a sifter. Sift the dry ingredients alternately with the sour milk into the creamed mixture. Mix well. Stir in chopped nuts.

Pour into prepared pan and bake at 350 degrees for about 45 minutes, or until edges pull away from sides of pan.

While cake is baking, prepare the topping. Blend the butter, honey, cream and nuts until well mixed. Spread the topping on the cake as soon as it is done. Place cake under broiler until topping browns slightly. Cool in pan on wire rack.

APPLESAUCE CAKE

Preheat oven to: 350 *degrees*
Utensils needed: 1 *9-inch loaf pan, greased and floured*
Baking time: 1 *hour*

1 *cup butter*
½ *cup brown sugar*
1 *teaspoon cinnamon*
1 *teaspoon ground cloves*
1 *teaspoon nutmeg*
2 *heaping cups sifted flour*
2 *teaspoons baking soda*
1 *cup seedless raisins*
1 *cup chopped walnuts*
1½ *cups sweetened applesauce*

Cream together the sugar, butter and spices until light and fluffy. Add the sifted flour and baking soda. Mix well. Stir in the raisins and nuts. Continue stirring while adding the applesauce. Mix well and pour into the prepared loaf pan.

Bake at 350 degrees for 1 hour or until edges pull away from sides of pan. Cool in pan on wire rack.

APPLESAUCE DATE CAKE

Preheat oven to: 350 *degrees*
Utensils needed: 2 *8-inch loaf pans, greased and floured*
Baking time: 45 *minutes*

6 *tablespoons softened butter*
1¼ *cups sugar*
1½ *cups applesauce, sugarless*
1 *cup pitted and finely chopped dates*
1 *cup chopped walnuts*
2 *teaspoons cinnamon*
1 *teaspoon ground cloves*
3 *cups sifted flour*
¼ *teaspoon salt*
2 *teaspoons baking soda*

Cream butter and sugar until light. Add the applesauce and mix well.

In a separate bowl, place the dates, nuts, cinnamon and cloves. Using ½ cup flour, dust the mixture and stir until the date pieces are separated. Set aside. Sift together the remaining 2½ cups of flour, the salt and the baking soda. Add to the creamed mixture. Mix well. Add the floured dates, nuts and spices to the batter. Mix well.

Pour into prepared pans and bake at 350 degrees for 45 minutes or until edges pull away from sides of pans. Remove from pans and cool on wire racks.

FILLED SOUR-CREAM CAKE

Preheat oven to: 375 *degrees*
Utensils needed: 1 *9-inch-square baking pan, greased and floured*
Baking time: 40 *minutes*

2 *cups sifted flour*
1 *teaspoon baking powder*
1 *teaspoon baking soda*
1 *cup butter*
1 *cup sugar*
2 *eggs*
1 *cup sour cream*

FILLING
½ *cup chopped nuts*
2 *tablespoons firmly packed brown sugar*
2 *teaspoons cinnamon*

Sift together the flour, baking powder and baking soda. In a separate bowl, cream together the butter and sugar until light and fluffy. Add eggs, beating thoroughly after each addition.

Into the creamed butter-sugar-egg mixture, blend the sifted dry ingredients alternately with the sour cream.

Pour half of the batter into prepared pan.

Mix the filling and sprinkle half on the batter. Pour in remaining batter and sprinkle remaining nut mixture over the top.

Bake at 375 degrees for about 40 minutes, or until edges pull away from sides of pan. Remove from pan and cool on wire rack.

PRUNE CAKE

Preheat oven to: 350 *degrees*
Utensils needed: 2 *9-inch cake pans, greased and floured* or 1 *8-inch-square pan, greased and floured*
Baking time: 45 *minutes*

¾ *cup softened butter*
2 *cups sugar*
1 *teaspoon baking soda*
1 *cup sour milk*
3 *cups sifted flour*
½ *teaspoon ground cloves*
½ *teaspoon cinnamon*
½ *teaspoon nutmeg*
2 *eggs*
1 *cup chopped nutmeats*
1½ *cups chopped cooked prunes*

Cream the butter and sugar until light and fluffy. Stir the baking soda into the sour milk and add it to the creamed butter-sugar mixture, alternately with the sifted flour. Add the spices and continue mixing. Add the eggs; mix well. Stir in the nutmeats and the prunes.

Pour into prepared pans and bake at 350 degrees for 45 minutes or until edges pull away from sides of pans. Remove from pans; cool on wire racks.

GINGERBREAD HOUSE

THE JOY and beauty of a Gingerbread House more than compensate for the amount of work involved in making one. Once you have created a house, you will want to make one every holiday season. To children, a Gingerbread House is a fairy tale come true, and to adults it is remembrances of Christmases long past.

The following steps will greatly aid you in planning and executing a successful Gingerbread House. Steps 2 and 5 can be family projects, while the other steps are best done by one person.

1. Using heavy cardboard, draw the pattern pieces for the house (see page 42). Be sure you measure carefully. Cut pieces

with a sharp knife, labeling each as you go. Place all pattern pieces in a secure place.

2. Purchase the candy, cookies and nonedible decorations you will need.

3. Allow three days for the making of the house. On the first day, make the dough, cut it to the pattern and bake it. All pieces should be handled very carefully and stored in a safe place.

4. On the second day, "glue" the house together. If you are going to display it on a tray, glue the house to it.

5. On the third day, decorate your house. And enjoy it!

GINGERBREAD HOUSE

Preheat oven to: 350 *degrees*
Utensils needed: At least 3 *rimless cookie sheets, greased*
Baking time: Approximately 12 *to* 15 *minutes for large pieces;* 5 *to* 7 *minutes for small pieces*

The following recipe must be made twice for a complete house. You will have enough dough left for Gingerbread Men or cookie decorations for the house.

1 *cup softened butter*
1 *cup light-brown sugar*
½ *cup molasses*
½ *cup dark corn syrup*
6 *cups sifted all-purpose flour*
1 *tablespoon grated lemon rind*
½ *teaspoon salt*
2 *teaspoons cinnamon*
1 *teaspoon nutmeg*
1 *teaspoon ginger*
½ *teaspoon mace*

Place the butter, brown sugar, molasses and corn syrup in a heavy saucepan over medium heat. Stir until all ingredients are melted. Keep warm.

Place the lemon rind in a large mixing bowl and resift the flour together with all other dry ingredients into the bowl.

Stir butter/syrup mixture into dry ingredients. Use your hands to combine, and knead thoroughly to incorporate the flour. This should produce a warm, firm mass of dough.

Place a large handful of dough on a greased rimless cookie sheet. Roll out to ⅛-inch thickness.

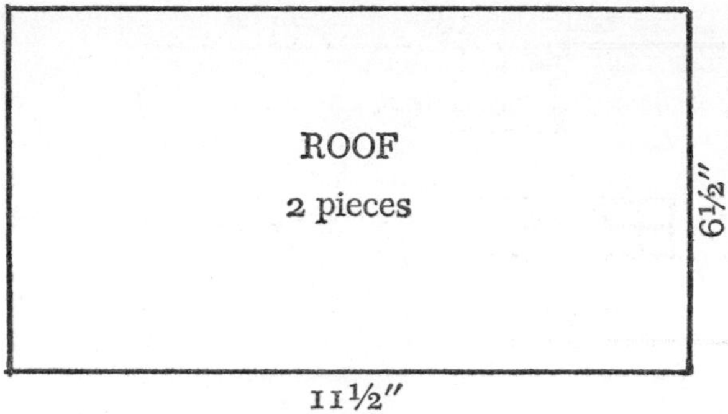
ROOF
2 pieces
6½″
11½″

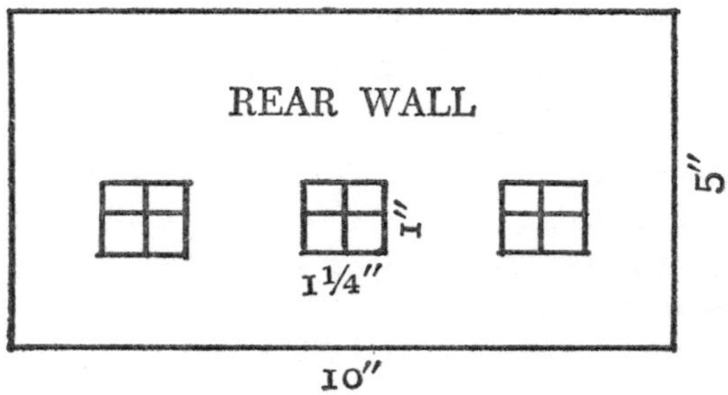
REAR WALL
1″
1¼″
5″
10″

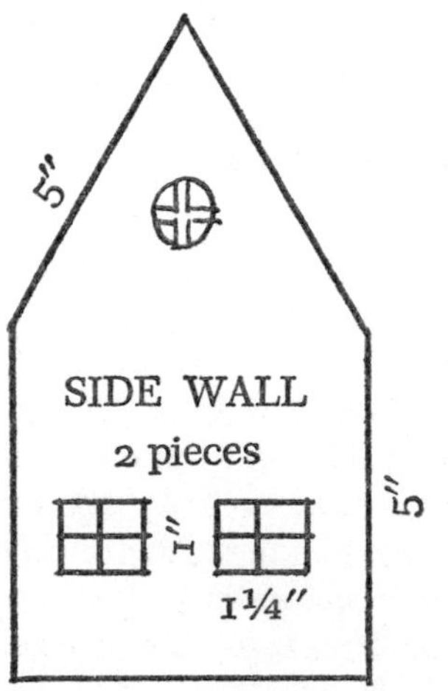
5″
SIDE WALL
2 pieces
1″
1¼″
5″

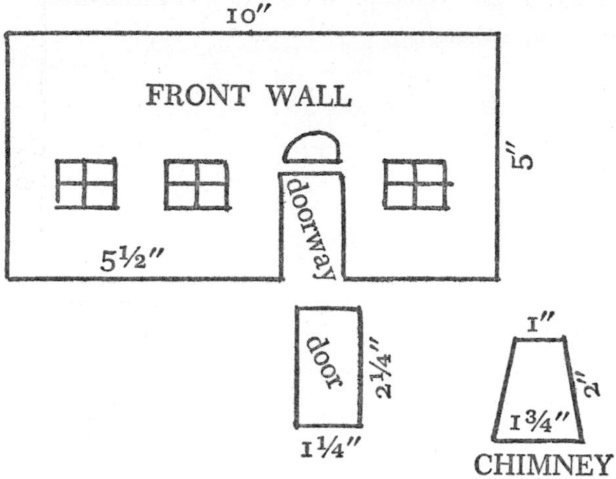

Dust cardboard pattern pieces lightly with flour. Place on dough and cut around them with a sharp knife. Remove left-over dough and save for further use. On wall pieces, cut out the windows with a small paring knife, and if you wish to make panes, form tiny strips of dough and fit into place.

When dough pieces are complete, chill for ½ hour before baking. Then bake in 350-degree oven for prescribed time or until firm and slightly browned at edges. Check from time to time during baking. If bubbles form, pat them down with a spatula, being careful not to tear dough.

Cool on pans until each piece is quite firm. Finish cooling on wire rack. Store securely until you are ready to build house.

TO ASSEMBLE HOUSE:

Melt 2 cups granulated sugar in a heavy skillet at least 12 inches across. Use very low heat to keep sugar from burning, and stir constantly until sugar is melted.

Starting with the walls, dip edges of the gingerbread pieces into the sugar-syrup glue. Work slowly. Make sure pieces are firmly stuck before adding on a new piece.

When the four walls are secure, dip a brush into the syrup glue and coat the tray on which you are going to place the house. Immediately set the frame on the prepared tray.

To place roof on house, dip inside edges, excluding the top edge, of one roof piece into syrup glue. Brush glue also on the slanting edges of end walls. Quickly set that half of roof in place, carefully lining up top edge with peak of side wall and leaving about ¾-inch overhang at each side edge. Make sure first half of roof is secure before gluing on the other half.

Drip glue along the top meeting edges of roof, and set the chimney piece about 2 inches in from one end in the crack formed by the meeting of the roof pieces.

Glue the door piece to one side of doorway, leaving it about half open.

To permit the glue to harden thoroughly, let the house sit undisturbed at least 24 hours before proceeding with the decoration.

SNOW ICING

1 *pound confectioner's sugar, sifted*
3 *egg whites, slightly beaten*
1 *teaspoon cream of tartar*
drop of white vinegar

Prepare one batch of Snow Icing at a time. You will probably need at least two batches to complete the decoration.

Place sugar in small bowl of electric mixer. Add the slightly beaten egg whites, and beat together on lowest speed of mixer for about 1 minute.

Add cream of tartar and drop of vinegar and beat on high speed of electric mixer until icing is stiff and shiny, as for meringue.

TO DECORATE HOUSE:

Spread Snow Icing liberally on the roof. Then immediately start setting candy or cookie trim in place on it. Any wafer-type cookies or nonpareils make excellent roof tiles.

With a finger, spread about ⅛ inch of icing around the window edges. Immediately decorate with small candy pieces to simulate shutters or paint trim.

Decorate the door and sides of house as you wish.

Cover the tray with Snow Icing and place any desired "lawn" decoration in the icing. These can be small plastic items of the dimestore variety or more candy or gingerbread-cookie trim.

2 · Breads

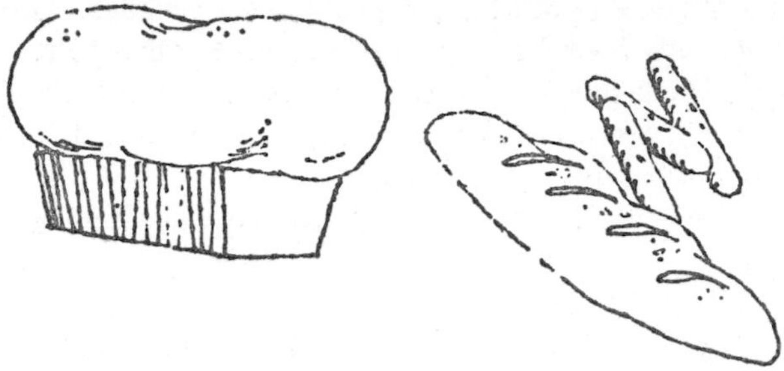

HOMEMADE BREAD is about the most unexpected treat that you can make for your family or friends. A gift of freshly made bread and a tub of homemade butter is something almost anyone will appreciate.

Most of the breads that we have chosen are "quick" breads—that is, breads made without yeast and quicker and easier to prepare than yeast breads. Quick breads are especially nice made in small (6 × 3-inch) loaf pans which can be ordered from a store listed in our Shopping Guide (page 192).

The yeast breads included are simple to make. If you have never made a yeast bread, your first loaf may be a disaster, but your next may be perfect. One of the most common errors in making yeast breads is dissolving the yeast in water either too hot or too cold. Use very warm water (105 to 115 degrees) for dry yeast, or lukewarm water (85 degrees) for compressed yeast. All other ingredients, unless otherwise specified, should be at room temperature. All breads are easily frozen and will keep, wrapped airtight in freezer wrap, for up to three months.

Breads may be wrapped for gift giving in much the same way as loaf cakes. They are especially attractive wrapped airtight in plastic wrap, then covered with colored cellophane.

You may also wish to give them in a plastic bread-storage container which can be purchased in housewares departments of most large stores or in five-and-ten-cent stores. An additional gift could be a breadboard or bread knife.

Homemade breads can be the basis for an assortment of homemade goodies such as jams, jellies, butter, spiced teas and/or mocha coffee. Packed in a decorated fruit basket or even a colorful shopping bag, this would be a most welcome gift on any occasion.

We have divided the recipes into three groups: yeast breads, tea breads and fruit breads. At the end of this section we have a recipe for homemade butter, which will go beautifully with any of them.

Yeast Breads

CUBAN BREAD

Utensils needed: 1 *baking sheet*
Baking time: 40 *to* 45 *minutes*
Quantity: 2 *loaves*

1 *package yeast*
2 *cups lukewarm water*
1¼ *tablespoons salt*
1 *tablespoon sugar*
6 *to* 7 *cups sifted flour*
cornmeal
sesame seed
boiling water

Dissolve yeast in lukewarm water in large mixing bowl. Add the salt and sugar and stir until dissolved. Add flour one cup at a time, beating well after each addition, until you have added enough to make a smooth dough.

Cover the dough with a towel and set in a warm place to rise until double in size, about 1½ hours. Then place on a floured board and shape into 2 loaves, either long or round.

Sprinkle baking sheet heavily with cornmeal. Place loaves on baking sheet and allow to rise for 5 minutes more. Slash the tops, brush with water and sprinkle with sesame seed.

Place in a *cold* oven, set the oven for 400 degrees and put a pan of boiling water on the bottom shelf. Bake at 400 degrees for 40 to 45 minutes, or until tops of loaves are lightly browned. Remove to wire racks to cool.

FRENCH BREAD

Preheat oven to: 375 *degrees*
Utensils needed: 2 *clean damp cloths, plus glasses to hold them as cloth tents over rising bread*
2 *greased cookie sheets, sprinkled with cornmeal*
Baking time: 40 *minutes*
Quantity: 2 *loaves*

2 *packages yeast*
2½ *cups lukewarm water*
2 *cups sifted flour*
1 *tablespoon salt*
5½ *cups sifted flour*
1 *egg white, slightly beaten*
1 *tablespoon water*

Mix the yeast into ½ cup lukewarm water.

In another bowl, sift together the flour and salt. Stir in the remaining 2 cups lukewarm water. Blend well. Add the dissolved yeast mixture. Blend together well. Stir in 4½ cups sifted flour. Cover tightly and let set for 10 minutes.

Then knead dough for 10 minutes, working in the remaining 1 cup sifted flour. Cover and let rise 1½ hours in a greased bowl set in a warm place.

Punch down dough and then let rise again for 1 hour as above. Divide dough into two parts. Cover each half with a deep bowl and let set again for 10 minutes.

Roll each half of dough as for a jelly roll. Starting at the narrow edge, tightly roll the dough into a French Bread shape.

Place each loaf on a prepared cookie sheet. With a sharp knife, make three slashes across the top of the loaf. Brush with egg white slightly beaten with water. Make a tent of a damp cloth, held up by several glasses, over each loaf; be sure that the cloth does not touch the dough. Let bread rise in a warm spot for 1½ hours.

Bake 20 minutes in 375-degree oven. Remove from oven and again brush the tops with egg white slightly beaten with water. Then bake another 20 minutes.

Cool on wire racks in a drafty spot—important so that bread will not be soggy.

QUICK WHITE BREAD

Preheat oven to: 425 *degrees*
Utensils needed: 4 *9-inch loaf pans, greased and floured*
Baking time: 15 *minutes at* 425 *degrees*–30 *minutes at* 375 *degrees*

2 *cups milk*
5 *tablespoons sugar*
2 *tablespoons salt*
2 *packages yeast*
2 *cups lukewarm water*
12 (*approximately*) *cups sifted flour*
5 *tablespoons melted shortening*

Scald together the milk, sugar and salt; cool to lukewarm. Dissolve yeast in 2 cups lukewarm water; add the lukewarm milk mixture. Stir in 6 cups sifted flour and beat until smooth. Add melted shortening and enough additional flour to produce an easily handled dough. Knead dough quickly and lightly until smooth and elastic. Place dough in greased bowl, cover and let rise in a warm place for 1½ hours.

When dough has risen, divide into 4 equal portions and shape into loaves. Place loaves in prepared pans, cover and let rise until double in bulk, about 1 hour.

Bake at 425 degrees for 15 minutes; then reduce heat to 375 degrees and finish baking, about 30 minutes. While loaves are still hot, rub tops with softened butter. Cool on wire racks after removing from pans.

SPICY SALT STICKS

Preheat oven to: 400 *degrees*
Utensils needed: 2 *greased cookie sheets, salted and seeded*
Baking time: 15 *to* 20 *minutes*
Quantity: 2 *dozen breadsticks*
Storing: These keep for a long time. Use an empty cereal box or plastic container, and place carefully so sticks remain unbroken

1 *package dry yeast*
1¼ *cups very warm water*
3 *tablespoons sugar*
1 *teaspoon salt*
4½ *teaspoons caraway seed*
1 *tablespoon butter*

¼ *teaspoon onion salt*
3½ *cups sifted flour*
2 *tablespoons kosher salt*

Dissolve yeast in 1¼ cups very warm water. Stir in sugar, 1 teaspoon salt, 2½ teaspoons caraway seed, butter and onion salt. Sift in flour and mix well. Place dough on lightly floured board and knead until smooth and elastic, about 10 minutes. Turn into greased bowl, turn dough once, cover and let rise in warm place until double in bulk, about 1 hour.

Punch dough down, place on floured board and divide in half. Roll each half into a rectangle 12 inches long. Then cut each half into 12 equal strips. Roll each strip with hands into a rope 12 inches long by ⅓ inch thick.

Place 1 teaspoon caraway seed and 1 tablespoon kosher salt on each greased cookie sheet. Roll each rope piece in caraway-salt mixture. Place dough sticks on cookie sheet. Cover and let rise 1 hour or until double in bulk.

Bake at 400 degrees for 15 to 20 minutes, or until lightly browned. Cool out of pan on wire racks. Handle carefully while warm.

Tea Breads

BOSTON BROWN BREAD

Preheat oven to: 350 *degrees*
Utensils needed: 6 *gold-lined No.* 303 *tin cans*
Baking time: 50 *minutes*

2 *cups boiling water*
½ *pound raisins*
2 *teaspoons baking soda*
2 *tablespoons butter*
2 *cups sugar*
2 *eggs*
4 *cups sifted flour*
1 *teaspoon salt*
2 *teaspoons vanilla*
1 *cup chopped walnuts*

In a bowl pour the boiling water over the raisins and baking soda. Mix together and let cool to room temperature.

Cream the butter and sugar together. Add the eggs and mix well. Add the flour, salt, vanilla and chopped nuts. Add the raisin mixture.

Fill the 6 cans about half full. Bake at 350 degrees for 50 minutes, or until breads pull away from sides of cans. When done, let stand in cans for 5 to 10 minutes. Then remove from cans and let cool completely on wire racks.

BUTTERMILK TEA BREAD

Preheat oven to: 350 *degrees*
Utensils needed: 1 *9-inch loaf pan, greased and floured*
Baking time: Approximately 45 *minutes*

2¼ *cups sifted flour*
2 *teaspoons baking powder*
½ *teaspoon salt*
½ *teaspoon baking soda*
½ *teaspoon cinnamon*
¼ *teaspoon nutmeg*
1 *cup brown sugar*
1 *egg, slightly beaten*
1 *cup chopped pecans*
1 *cup buttermilk*
2 *tablespoons melted butter*

Sift together the flour, baking powder, salt, baking soda, cinnamon, nutmeg and sugar.

In another bowl combine the egg, nuts, buttermilk and melted butter. Add this to the flour mixture. Mix until just moistened.

Pour into prepared pan. Bake at 350 degrees for about 45 minutes, or until lightly browned. Cool about 10 minutes before removing from pan. Place on wire rack to finish cooling.

MARMALADE TEA BREAD

Preheat oven to: 350 *degrees*
Utensils needed: 1 *9-inch loaf pan, greased and floured*
Baking time: 1 *hour*

3 *cups sifted flour*
3 *teaspoons baking powder*
1 *teaspoon salt*
1 *1-pound jar orange marmalade*
1 *egg*

¾ cup orange juice
¼ cup salad oil
1 cup coarsely chopped walnuts

Sift together the flour, baking powder and salt. Remove ¼ cup marmalade and set aside. Combine remaining marmalade, egg, orange juice and salad oil. Add this to the sifted dry ingredients and stir until moistened. Stir in nuts.

Place mixture in prepared pan. Bake at 350 degrees for 1 hour or until lightly browned. When bread is done, remove from pan and place on baking sheet. Spread the remaining marmalade over the top and return to the oven for about 1 minute to glaze. Remove from pan and place on wire rack.

PUMPKIN TEA BREAD

Preheat oven to: 325 *degrees*
Utensils needed: 2 *9-inch loaf pans, greased and floured*
Baking time: Approximately 1 *hour*

2 cups sugar
1 cup vegetable oil
3 eggs, lightly beaten
2 cups canned pumpkin
3 cups sifted flour
¾ teaspoon salt
1 teaspoon baking soda
¾ teaspoon baking powder
2 teaspoons cinnamon
1½ teaspoons nutmeg
1 teaspoon ground cloves
½ teaspoon mace

Blend the sugar and oil well with an electric mixer. Then, as you continue beating, add the eggs one at a time, and beat until light. Add the pumpkin. Mix well. Sift the flour, salt, baking soda, baking powder and spices into the creamed mixture. Beat at low speed until blended.

Pour batter into prepared pans and bake at 325 degrees for approximately 1 hour, or until lightly browned. When done, leave in pans for 15 minutes; then remove from pans and cool on wire racks.

BUTTERSCOTCH TEA BREAD

Preheat oven to: 350 *degrees*
Utensils needed: 1 *9-inch loaf pan, greased and floured*
Baking time: Approximately 1 *hour*

1 *egg, lightly beaten*
1 *cup brown sugar, firmly packed*
1 *tablespoon softened butter*
2 *cups flour*
¾ *teaspoon baking soda*
½ *teaspoon baking powder*
¼ *teaspoon salt*
1 *cup buttermilk*
1 *cup broken pecan meats*

Beat together thoroughly the egg, brown sugar and butter. Sift together the flour, baking soda, baking powder and salt. Add to egg mixture alternately with the buttermilk. Stir in nuts.

Pour into prepared pan and bake at 350 degrees for about 1 hour, or until lightly browned. Remove from pan and cool on wire rack.

WHOLE-WHEAT TEA BREAD

Preheat oven to: 350 *degrees*
Utensils needed: 1 *8-inch loaf pan, greased and floured*
Baking time: 55 *minutes*

1 *cup sifted flour*
2 *teaspoons baking powder*
¼ *teaspoon salt*
½ *teaspoon cinnamon*
¼ *teaspoon nutmeg*
¼ *teaspoon allspice*
½ *cup whole-wheat flour*
¼ *cup butter*
¾ *cup sugar*
2 *eggs*
⅔ *cup milk*
½ *teaspoon vanilla*
½ *cup chopped walnuts*

Sift together flour, baking powder, salt, cinnamon, nutmeg and allspice. Stir in whole-wheat flour.

In a separate bowl, cream together the butter and sugar. Add the eggs separately, beating well after each addition.

Add the sifted dry ingredients alternately with the milk and vanilla to the creamed butter mixture. Beat well. Stir in nuts. Pour into prepared pan.

Bake at 350 degrees for 55 minutes or until lightly browned. Cool 10 minutes and remove from pan. Place on wire rack.

Fruit Breads

APRICOT BREAD

Preheat oven to: 350 *degrees*
Utensils needed: 1 *9-inch loaf pan, greased and floured*
Baking time: Approximately 50 *minutes*

½ *cup chopped and cooked dried apricots*
½ *cup seedless raisins*
grated rind of 1 *large orange*
juice of 1 *large orange*
boiling water
1 *teaspoon baking soda*
¾ *cup sugar*
2 *tablespoons melted butter*
1 *teaspoon vanilla*
1 *egg, lightly beaten*
2¼ *cups sifted flour*
¼ *teaspoon salt*
2 *teaspoons baking powder*
¾ *cup chopped nutmeats*

Place apricots, raisins and grated rind in mixing bowl. Place orange juice in measuring cup and add boiling water to make 1 cup liquid. Add to fruit. Stir in baking soda, sugar, melted butter and vanilla. Stir in beaten egg. Sift in remaining dry ingredients and stir. Blend in nutmeats.

Pour into prepared pan and bake at 350 degrees for about 50 minutes, or until lightly browned. Turn upside down on wire rack to cool.

BETTYE'S FAVORITE BANANA BREAD

Preheat oven to: 350 *degrees*
Utensils needed: 1 *9-inch loaf pan, greased and floured*
Baking time: Approximately 1 *hour*

⅓ *cup softened butter*
⅔ *cup sugar*
2 *eggs*
3 *mashed bananas*
1¾ *cups sifted flour*
2 *teaspoons baking powder*
¼ *teaspoon baking soda*
½ *teaspoon salt*
1 *teaspoon vanilla*
1 *cup large walnut pieces*

Cream the butter and sugar until light and fluffy. Add eggs and beat well. Add the bananas. Blend well.

Sift together the flour, baking powder, baking soda and salt. Gradually add to the batter. Mix well. Stir in the vanilla and the walnuts.

Pour into prepared pan and bake at 350 degrees for about 1 hour, or until lightly browned. Remove from pan and cool on wire rack.

CURRANT BREAD

Preheat oven to: 350 *degrees*
Utensils needed: 1 *9-inch loaf pan, greased and floured*
Baking time: 1 *hour*

1 *cup butter*
1 *cup white* or *brown sugar*
3 *eggs*
3 *cups sifted flour*
1 *teaspoon baking powder*
½ *teaspoon baking soda*
½ *teaspoon salt*
1 *teaspoon nutmeg*
1 *teaspoon cinnamon*
1¼ *cups buttermilk*
1 *cup raisins*
1 *cup currants*
1 *cup chopped walnuts*

Cream the butter and sugar together. Beat in the eggs. Sift 2¾ cups flour with the other dry ingredients and add to the creamed butter-sugar mixture. Stir in the buttermilk.

Dredge the fruit and nuts with the remaining ¼ cup of flour

and fold in. We find mixing with our hands an easy way to do this. Spread the batter into prepared pan. Bake at 350 degrees for 1 hour or until lightly browned. Let cool in pan 5 minutes, remove and place on wire rack to finish cooling.

ORANGE-CRANBERRY BREAD

Preheat oven to: 350 *degrees*
Utensils needed: 1 *9-inch loaf pan, greased and floured*
Baking time: 50 *minutes*

2 *cups sifted flour*
¾ *cup sugar*
1½ *teaspoons baking powder*
1 *teaspoon salt*
½ *teaspoon baking soda*
1 *cup coarsely chopped cranberries*
½ *cup chopped walnuts*
1 *teaspoon grated orange peel*
1 *egg*
¾ *cup orange juice*
2 *tablespoons salad oil*

Sift together the flour, sugar, baking powder, salt and baking soda. Stir in cranberries, nuts and orange peel. In another bowl combine the egg, orange juice and salad oil. Add to the flour-fruit mixture. Stir until just moistened.

Pour into prepared pan. Bake at 350 degrees for 50 minutes, or until lightly browned. Remove from pan and cool on wire rack.

ANNIE'S ORANGE-NUT BREAD

Preheat oven to: 350 *degrees*
Utensils needed: 1 *9-inch loaf pan, greased and floured*
Baking time: Approximately 55 *minutes*

1 *cup finely chopped orange peel*
2¼ *cups sifted enriched flour*
¾ *cup sugar*
1 *tablespoon baking powder*
1 *teaspoon salt*
1 *cup chopped walnuts*
2 *beaten eggs*
1 *cup milk*
3 *tablespoons butter, melted*

To prepare orange peel: With a sharp knife, cut peel from 2 very large oranges into thin strips. Lay several strips together on cutting board and chop fine. You may need an extra orange.

Sift together flour, sugar, baking powder and salt. Add orange peel and chopped walnuts.

In a separate bowl, combine eggs, milk and melted butter. Add the egg mixture to the dry ingredients quickly, stirring just until flour is moistened.

Pour into prepared pan and bake at 350 degrees for about 55 minutes, or until lightly browned. Remove from pan and cool on wire rack.

SUPER DATE-NUT BREAD

Preheat oven to: 325 *degrees*
Utensils needed: 3 *6-inch loaf pans, greased and floured*
Baking time: 10 *minutes at* 325 *degrees; approximately* 30 *minutes at* 350 *degrees*

1 *pound whole pitted dates*
1 *teaspoon baking soda*
1¼ *cups boiling water*
1 *tablespoon butter*
¾ *cup sugar*
1 *egg, lightly beaten*
¼ *teaspoon salt*
1 *teaspoon vanilla*
2 *cups sifted flour*
1½ *cups large walnut pieces*

Place dates in mixing bowl. Sprinkle with the soda. Pour the boiling water over the dates. Stir. Add the butter and mix until it melts. Stir in the sugar. Mix until it begins to dissolve. Add the lightly beaten egg, salt and vanilla. Mix well. Sift in the 2 cups sifted flour and beat well with a wooden spoon. Stir in the walnut pieces.

Pour batter into prepared pans. Bake at 325 degrees for the first 10 minutes; then raise oven temperature to 350 degrees and continue baking for about 30 minutes more.

Remove from pans and cool on wire racks.

PINEAPPLE BREAD

Preheat oven to: 350 *degrees*
Utensils needed: 1 9-*inch loaf pan, greased and floured*
Baking time: Approximately 50 *minutes*

½ *cup softened butter*
1⅓ *cups sugar*
3 *egg yolks, lightly beaten*
2¼ *cups sifted* cake *flour*
3 *teaspoons baking powder*
½ *teaspoon salt*
1 *cup heavy cream*
½ *cup milk*
3 *egg whites, stiffly beaten*
1 *cup chopped nutmeats*
¼ *cup drained crushed pineapple*

Cream the butter and sugar together until light. Add the beaten egg yolks and mix in well.

Sift the flour, baking powder and salt together; add alternately with the heavy cream and milk to the creamed mixture.

Fold the stiffly beaten egg whites into the batter. Lightly fold in nutmeats and drained pineapple.

Pour into prepared pan and bake at 350 degrees for about 50 minutes, or until lightly browned. Remove to wire rack to cool.

CANDIED-FRUIT BREAD

Preheat oven to: 350 *degrees*
Utensils needed: 1 8-*inch loaf pan, greased and floured*
Baking time: 50 *minutes*

1 *cup butter*
¾ *cup sugar*
6 *eggs*
2 *cups sifted flour*
1 *teaspoon baking powder*
1 *cup candied fruit* or
½ *cup candied fruit* plus
½ *cup chopped walnuts*

Cream the butter and sugar together thoroughly. Add the eggs, one at a time, beating well after each addition.

Sift together the flour and baking powder. Mix ¼ cup of the

flour mixture into the fruit or fruit and nuts in a separate bowl.

Fold the remaining flour mixture into the creamed butter-sugar mixture. Add the floured fruit or fruit-nut combination and fold into the mixture.

Pour into prepared pan. Bake at 350 degrees for 50 minutes or until lightly browned. Remove from pan and cool on wire rack.

PRUNE BREAD

Preheat oven to: 350 *degrees*
Utensils needed: 1 *9-inch loaf pan, greased and floured*
Baking time: 50 *to* 60 *minutes*

1¼ *cups flour*
1 *cup sugar*
½ *teaspoon salt*
1 *teaspoon baking powder*
1 *teaspoon baking soda*
1 *cup bran flakes*
1 *cup chopped nuts*
1 *egg*
1 *cup sour cream*
½ *cup prune juice*
2 *tablespoons melted butter*
½ *cup chopped cooked prunes*
½ *teaspoon instant-coffee powder*

Sift together flour, sugar, salt, baking powder and baking soda. Add bran flakes and nuts. Blend together.

Beat the egg with the sour cream and add the prune juice, melted butter, prunes and instant-coffee powder. Stir into sifted dry ingredients and mix well.

Pour into prepared pan and bake at 350 degrees for 50 to 60 minutes, or until lightly browned. Remove from pan and cool on wire rack.

HOMEMADE BUTTER

Utensils needed: Electric blender
Quantity: About 1 *cup (approximately* ½ *pound)*

1 *cup heavy cream*
½ *cup ice water*
2 *large ice cubes, chopped*
salt to taste, if desired

Place cream in electric blender. Cover and whip at highest speed. When cream is whipped, add water and chopped ice cubes. Cover and blend at highest speed at least 2 minutes, or until all cream has turned to butter particles.

Pour contents of blender into a sieve to drain. When all water has drained through, place butter in a small bowl. Add salt, if desired, and knead with a wooden spoon until butter is smooth. Place in covered butter crock or plastic container in the refrigerator.

NOTE: For variety, you may add to the butter a clove of garlic, a tablespoon of grated orange or lemon peel or a small quantity of any ground herb you wish. Add the flavoring when you add the water and ice.

3 · Cookies

THERE IS nothing friendlier than a filled cookie jar given as a gift. Almost everyone has a favorite cookie, but we hope that you will find new favorites among the recipes we have included here.

Cookies are usually the easiest of homemade goodies. The new Teflon cookie sheets make baking quicker and cleaner than ever. If you don't use these, you can line other types with greased aluminum foil, which can be prepared in advance. If you follow the directions closely and use prepared baking sheets, you will find cookie baking a breeze.

An assortment of cookie cutters and a cookie press will greatly enhance your repertoire. Most dime stores carry these, usually with an emphasis on holiday shapes. You can order any one of a large variety of cookie cutters from stores listed in our Shopping Guide (page 192), or you can make your own patterns using heavy cardboard. Illustrations in children's coloring books offer a variety of ideas for cookie shapes. Different-sized jars, glasses or lids can be used. You can even cut out the shape of your hand.

Most of our cookie recipes call for butter. You can, of course, substitute margarine, but this will change the taste, and occasionally the texture, of your cookie. For some cookies this will not matter, but rich cookies (those with few ingredients beyond butter, sugar and flour) demand the strong butter flavor. If you wish to see which you prefer, Shortbread is the best cookie to experiment with; margarine, sweet butter and salt butter will give you three entirely different results. Cookies made with margarine tend to keep longer than those made with butter.

Most cookies are lifted from the baking sheet immediately upon removal from the oven. They are best cooled on wire cake racks. The exception is bar cookies, which are cut and cooled directly in their baking pan. If you use a disposable foil baking pan, bar cookies may also be given as a gift while still in the pan.

Unless otherwise specified, cookies may be frozen either unbaked or baked. (Exception: It is best not to freeze dough made with vegetable oil, as freezing seems to make the dough crumbly.) Pressed or cutout cookies may be formed into the desired shapes, frozen on a cookie sheet, then removed and placed in layers in freezer wrap or a plastic bag for further freezer storage. Thaw unbaked dough thoroughly before using. Frozen baked cookies should be placed to thaw on paper toweling so that the moisture will be absorbed and the cookies will remain crisp.

A batch of homemade cookies to be given as a gift can be placed in almost any covered container. If they are packed in a box, it is best to place them in layers separated by tissue, foil, waxed paper or cellophane. Brightly colored tissue paper is a festive addition. A fruitcake tin or any reusable plastic container can be made into an attractive package. A large coffee can (or any large can with a plastic lid) can be painted and decorated with stick-on decals or covered with adhesive-backed decorating paper and used as a cookie container. Restaurant-sized mayonnaise or pickle jars make superb cookie jars when decorated.

Innumerable kitchen utensils can be purchased to serve as containers for cookie gifts: a large colander, a flour sifter, cookie sheets, mixing bowls—anything large enough to hold at least 1 pound of cookies. These are wonderful items for a young housewife or a bachelor or for shower gifts. A set of mixing bowls filled with cookies and wrapped in colored cellophane with a wooden spoon, a pastry brush or a spatula tied in the ribbon makes a charming gift package. If you are an antique- or junk-shop browser, you can always find old crocks or jars that are great for cookies.

For most children, homemade cookies are a special treat. A sandpail, a lunch box or a plastic dump truck is an inexpensive and appropriate container for a cookie gift to a child. This kind of gift is particularly appealing to a child recuperating from an illness.

All the cookie recipes given are good keepers. If you plan to send a batch of cookies through the mail, do not select those that are marked fragile. Check page 190 for additional hints on mailing cookies.

We have divided the cookies into six categories: Bar, Drop, Molded, Refrigerator, Cookie-Press and Cutout. At the end of this section we have included a recipe for Icing which may be used on any cookie that calls for decoration (see page 83).

Bar Cookies

DATE LOGS

Preheat oven to: 350 *degrees*
Utensils needed: 1 13 × 9 × 2*-inch pan, greased and floured*
Baking time: About 25 *minutes*
Quantity: 6 *dozen*
Storing: Individually plastic-wrapped in airtight container for 2 *weeks*

3 *eggs*
1 *cup sugar*
1½ *tablespoons orange juice*
1 *teaspoon lemon juice*
¾ *cup sifted flour*
½ *teaspoon baking powder*
¼ *teaspoon salt*
1 8*-ounce package pitted dates, chopped*
¼ *cup chopped candied orange peel*
1 *cup chopped walnuts*
granulated sugar

Beat eggs until foamy and light. Gradually add the sugar and continue beating until fluffy and thick. Stir in the fruit juices.

Sift together the flour, baking powder and salt and fold into the egg mixture. Gently fold in the dates, peel and nuts, making sure all ingredients are blended. Pour into prepared pan and spread evenly.

Bake at 350 degrees for about 25 minutes, or until toothpick inserted comes out clean. Cool in pan on wire rack at least 15 minutes. While still warm, cut lengthwise into 9 strips and crosswise into 8 strips, making 72 pieces. Remove from pan, one at a time, and roll logs in granulated sugar. Finish cooling on wire rack.

EASY LEBKUCHEN

Preheat oven to: 375 *degrees*
Utensils needed: 2 *cookie sheets, greased*
Baking time: 25 *minutes*
Quantity: 6 *dozen*
Storing: Airtight container for 4 *weeks*

4 *eggs*
1 *pound light-brown sugar*
2 *cups sifted flour*
1 *teaspoon cinnamon*
6 *ounces finely chopped pecans*
2 *ounces finely chopped citron*
1 *ounce finely chopped candied orange peel*

Beat the eggs with the sugar until light.

Mix flour and cinnamon with nuts, citron and orange peel. Combine flour mixture with egg mixture, blending well.

Spread dough onto prepared cookie sheets. Bake at 375 degrees for 25 minutes or until lightly browned. When cooled, cut into strips approximately 5 inches × 1 inch.

GUMDROP COOKIES

Preheat oven to: 350 *degrees*
Utensils needed: 2 13 × 9-*inch pans, greased and floured*
Baking time: About 30 *minutes*
Quantity: About 5 *dozen*
Storing: Airtight container for 10 *days*

2 *cups brown sugar*
3 *egg yolks*
4 *teaspoons water*
2 *cups sifted flour*
1 *tablespoon cinnamon*
1 *cup chopped gumdrops*
3 *egg whites, stiffly beaten*
confectioner's sugar

Beat the brown sugar and egg yolks until light and well blended. Stir in the water. Sift in the flour and cinnamon. Mix well. Stir in the chopped gumdrops. Fold in the stiffly beaten egg whites.

Pour batter into prepared pans and bake at 350 degrees for about 30 minutes, or until toothpick inserted comes out clean.

Cool slightly in pans. Cut into squares (no larger than 2 × 2 inches). Remove from pans, dust with confectioner's sugar and finish cooling on wire racks.

EDNA'S BROWNIES

Preheat oven to: 350 *degrees*
Utensils needed: 1 *8-inch-square pan, greased and floured*
Baking time: About 25 *minutes*
Quantity: About 3 *dozen*
Storing: Individually plastic-wrapped in airtight container for 10 *days*

½ *cup butter*
1 *cup sugar*
2 *eggs*
1 *teaspoon vanilla*
½ *cup sifted flour*
4 *tablespoons cocoa*
1 *teaspoon salt*
¼ *cup chopped walnuts*

Cream the butter and sugar until light and fluffy. Beat in the eggs and vanilla.

Sift the flour, cocoa and salt into the creamed mixture. Mix well. Stir in the chopped nuts and pour into prepared pan.

Bake at 350 degrees for about 25 minutes, or until toothpick inserted comes out clean. Cut into squares while still warm, but leave in pan until cold.

PRALINE COOKIES

Preheat oven to: 325 *degrees*
Utensils needed: 1 *cookie sheet, greased*
Baking time: 25 *minutes*
Quantity: Approximately 3 *dozen*
Storing: Individually plastic-wrapped in loosely covered container for 10 *days*

½ *cup butter*
1 *egg*
1 *teaspoon vanilla*
1½ *cups brown sugar*
1½ *cups sifted flour*
1 *cup coarsely chopped pecans*

Cream together butter and sugar until light and fluffy. Add the egg and mix thoroughly. Add the vanilla, flour and nuts. Mix well.

Spread the mixture over the prepared pan with a spatula, extending the dough as closely to the edges of the pan as possible. Bake at 325 degrees for 25 minutes or until lightly browned. When cool, cut into squares.

Drop Cookies

ANISE CAPS

Preheat oven to: 350 *degrees*
Utensils needed: At least 2 *cookie sheets, generously greased*
Setting time: At least 12 *hours*
Baking time: 5 *to* 6 *minutes*
Quantity: About 4 *dozen*
Storing: Uncovered container for 2 *weeks. Do not freeze or refrigerate.*

2 *eggs*
1 *cup sugar*
¼ *teaspoon anise extract*
1½ *cups sifted flour*
¼ *teaspoon baking powder*
anise seed for cookie tops

Beat eggs until foamy. Gradually add the sugar and beat until very thick. When the mixture piles softly, add the anise extract. Sift the dry ingredients into the egg mixture and blend lightly.

Drop by the teaspoon 1–1½ inches apart onto the prepared pans. Sprinkle the top of each cookie with a small amount of anise seed.

Important: Before baking, these cookies must set at least 12 hours in a cool place. Do not cover them, and do not place them in the refrigerator.

When cookies have set, bake at 350 degrees for about 5 or 6 minutes, or until faintly brown. Remove from pan and cool on wire racks.

CHRISTMAS HERMITS

Preheat oven to: 375 *degrees*
Utensils needed: At least 2 *cookie sheets, greased*
Baking time: About 20 *minutes*
Quantity: About 10 *dozen*
Storing: Airtight container for 3 *weeks*

1 *cup softened butter*
3 *cups brown sugar*
4 *tablespoons milk*
4 *eggs*
3 *teaspoons baking powder*
6 *cups sifted flour*
2 *cups seedless raisins*
2 *cups currants*
1 *cup chopped nutmeats*
grated rind of 1 *medium orange*
1 *teaspoon nutmeg*
1 *teaspoon cinnamon*

Cream butter and sugar until light and fluffy. Beat in milk and eggs.

Sift the baking powder with 3 cups of the flour. Add to the creamed mixture. Blend well. Add the raisins, currants, nutmeats and orange rind and mix well.

Sift spices with the balance of the flour and add to the mixture. Blend together.

Drop by the teaspoonful 1–1½ inches apart onto prepared cookie sheets. Bake at 375 degrees for about 20 minutes, or until light brown. Remove from pan and cool on wire racks.

CRYBABIES

Preheat oven to: 350 *degrees*
Utensils needed: At least 2 *cookie sheets, greased*
Baking time: 12 *to* 15 *minutes*
Quantity: About 6 *dozen*
Storing: Loosely covered container for 10 *days*

1 *cup softened butter*
1 *cup sugar*
1 *cup molasses*
2½ *cups sifted flour (more if needed)*
2 *teaspoons cinnamon*

½ teaspoon ground ginger
¼ teaspoon salt
1 cup strong hot coffee
2 teaspoons baking soda
1 cup seedless dark raisins
1 cup chopped walnuts

Cream butter and sugar until light and fluffy. Beat in the molasses.

Sift together the flour, cinnamon, ginger and salt. Add to creamed mixture alternately with the hot coffee, in which you have dissolved 2 teaspoons baking soda. Stir in the raisins and nuts. Drop by the teaspoonful 1–1½ inches apart onto prepared cookie sheets. Bake at 350 degrees for 12 to 15 minutes, or until lightly browned. Remove from pan and cool on wire racks.

JUNE'S FRUIT COOKIES

Preheat oven to: 325 *degrees*
Utensils needed: At least 2 *cookie sheets, greased*
Baking time: About 12 *minutes*
Quantity: About 7 *dozen*
Storing: In airtight container, wrapped in a brandied cheesecloth, for 6 *weeks*

1 pound pitted dates, quartered
½ pound candied cherry halves
3 slices candied pineapple, chopped
½ pound chopped almonds
1 pound chopped Brazil nuts
2½ cups sifted flour
1 cup softened butter
1½ cups brown sugar, tightly packed
2 eggs
1 teaspoon cinnamon
½ teaspoon nutmeg
1 teaspoon baking soda
1 teaspoon salt

Place the dates, cherries, pineapple and nuts in a bowl and sift ½ cup flour over them. Mix well. Set aside.

Cream the butter and sugar until light and fluffy. Beat in the eggs. Sift the remaining 2 cups of flour and other dry ingredients into the creamed mixture, blending well. Fold in the floured fruits and nuts.

Drop by the teaspoonful onto prepared cookie sheets. Bake at 325 degrees for about 12 minutes, or until lightly browned. Remove from pan and cool on wire racks.

LIZZIES

Preheat oven to: 325 *degrees*
Utensils needed: At least 2 *cookie sheets, greased*
Baking time: About 15 *minutes*
Quantity: 8 *dozen*
Storing: Airtight container for 3 *weeks*

- 3 *cups seedless dark raisins*
- ½ *cup bourbon (or orange juice)*
- ¼ *cup softened butter*
- ½ *cup brown sugar*
- 2 *eggs*
- 1½ *cups sifted flour*
- 1 *teaspoon baking soda*
- 1½ *teaspoons cinnamon*
- ½ *teaspoon nutmeg*
- ½ *teaspoon ground cloves*
- 1 *pound whole pecan halves*
- ½ *pound diced citron*
- 1 *pound whole candied red cherries*

Place the raisins and bourbon (or orange juice) in a bowl. Stir and set aside for 1 hour.

Cream the butter and sugar until light and fluffy. Add the eggs; beat until well blended and fluffy. Sift together the flour, baking soda and spices. Add gradually to the creamed mixture alternately with the raisin mixture. Stir in the pecans, citron and cherries. Blend well.

Drop by the teaspoonful onto prepared cookie sheets. Bake at 325 degrees for 15 minutes, or until lightly browned. Remove from pan and cool on wire racks.

Molded Cookies

CHOCOLATE PIXIES

Preheat oven to: 375 *degrees*
Utensils needed: At least 2 *cookie sheets, greased*
Chilling time: ½ *hour*
Baking time: About 12 *minutes*

Quantity: About 4 dozen
Storing: Airtight container for 2 weeks

4 *squares unsweetened chocolate, melted*
½ *cup butter*
1½ *cups sugar*
2 *teaspoons vanilla*
4 *eggs*
2 *cups sifted flour*
2 *teaspoons baking powder*
½ *teaspoon salt*
½ *cup chopped pecans*
confectioner's sugar

Melt the chocolate in top of double boiler and let cool.

Cream the butter, sugar and vanilla until light and fluffy. Beat in the eggs. Continue beating and add the cool, melted chocolate.

Sift together the flour, baking powder and salt. Add to the creamed mixture and blend thoroughly. Stir in the chopped pecans. Chill about ½ hour.

When chilled, roll dough into 1-inch balls. Roll each ball in confectioner's sugar.

Place on prepared cookie sheets at least 2 inches apart. Bake at 375 degrees for about 12 minutes, or until lightly browned. Cool slightly on cookie sheets. Remove and finish cooling on wire racks.

FINGERS

Preheat oven to: 300 *degrees*
Utensils needed: At least 2 *cookie sheets, greased*
Baking time: 20 *to* 25 *minutes*
Quantity: About 7 *dozen*
Storing: Airtight container for 2 *weeks*

1 *cup softened sweet butter*
1 *cup sugar*
1 *cup finely ground hazelnuts (or almonds)*
2 *cups sifted flour*
¼ *teaspoon salt*
1½ *teaspoons vanilla*
confectioner's sugar

Cream butter and sugar until light and fluffy. Work in the nuts, flour, salt and vanilla with a pastry blender or your fingers.

Work with hands until dough holds together. If mixture is not holding, add about 1 tablespoon of ice water.

Shape each heaping teaspoon of dough into a "finger" by rolling on a board or between your palms. Place fingers on prepared cookie sheets at least 2 inches apart.

Bake at 300 degrees for 20 to 25 minutes, or until lightly browned. Place baked cookies on sheet of waxed paper or foil, dust with confectioner's sugar and cool on wire racks.

PEPPERMINT CRISPS

Preheat oven to: 350 *degrees*
Utensils needed: At least 2 *cookie sheets, greased*
Baking time: 8 *to* 10 *minutes*
Quantity: 2½ *dozen*
Storing: Airtight container for 10 *days*

¼ *cup butter*
½ *cup sugar*
1 *egg*
1 *cup sifted flour*
½ *teaspoon baking powder*
¼ *teaspoon baking soda*
¼ *teaspoon salt*
¼ *teaspoon nutmeg*
1 *tablespoon milk*
3 *to* 4 *tablespoons crushed peppermint-stick candy*

This recipe may be doubled.

Cream the butter and sugar until light and fluffy. Beat in the egg. Sift all dry ingredients together; add to the creamed mixture alternately with the milk. Mix well.

Drop by the teaspoonful onto the prepared cookie sheets, about 2½ inches apart. Press with bottom of a glass, dipped in flour to flatten. Sprinkle each cookie with crushed peppermint-stick candy.

Bake at 350 degrees for 8 to 10 minutes, or until lightly browned. Cool slightly before removing from cookie sheet. Finish cooling on wire racks.

GREEK KOURABIEDES

Preheat oven to: 350 *degrees*
Utensils needed: At least 2 *cookie sheets, greased*
Baking time: Approximately 18 *minutes*
Quantity: About 4 *dozen*
Storing: Airtight container for 1 *week, or refrigerated for longer storage*

1 *pound sweet butter, at room temperature*
¾ *cup unsifted confectioner's sugar*
1 *egg yolk*
1½ *tablespoons brandy*
4 *cups sifted flour*
confectioner's sugar

Cream butter until it is extremely light. Add ¾ cup confectioner's sugar and beat until mixture is very fluffy and pale in color. Beat in egg yolk and brandy.

Gradually add flour. Blend to make a soft dough that will shape into balls without sticking to your hands. Make the balls about 1 inch in diameter and place on prepared cookie sheets about 2 inches apart.

Bake at 350 degrees for about 18 minutes, or until lightly browned. Cool slightly on cookie sheet; then transfer to waxed paper and dust with confectioner's sugar. Finish cooling on wire racks.

WEDDING CAKES

Preheat oven to: 350 *degrees*
Utensils needed: 1 *cookie sheet, greased*
Baking time: 15 *to* 20 *minutes*
Quantity: 3 *dozen*
Storing: Individually plastic-wrapped in airtight container for 5 *days*

½ *pound butter, melted*
8 *tablespoons confectioner's sugar*
2 *cups sifted flour*
2 *cups chopped pecans or walnuts*
1 *teaspoon vanilla*
confectioner's sugar

Mix together melted butter and 8 tablespoons sugar. Add flour, nuts and vanilla. Roll into teaspoon-sized balls. Place on cookie sheet and bake at 350 degrees for 15 to 20 minutes, or until lightly browned. While still warm, roll each ball in confectioner's sugar. Cool on wire racks.

Refrigerator Cookies

SPICE COOKIES

Chilling time: 12 *or more hours*
Preheat oven to: 325 *degrees*
Utensils needed: 2 *cookie sheets, greased*
Baking time: 10 *to* 15 *minutes*
Quantity: 10 *dozen*
Storing: Plastic bags tied, for 2 *weeks*

1 *cup brown sugar*
1 *cup white sugar*
1½ *cups melted shortening*
3 *eggs*
1 *cup chopped nuts*
4⅓ *cups sifted flour*
2 *teaspoons baking soda*
1 *teaspoon salt*
1 *teaspoon cinnamon*
½ *teaspoon ground cloves*
½ *teaspoon nutmeg*

Mix together the brown and white sugars and melted shortening. Add eggs one at a time, mixing thoroughly after each addition. Add chopped nuts.

Sift together flour, baking soda, salt and spices. Add sifted dry ingredients to sugar-shortening mixture and blend well.

Form dough into long rolls and wrap in waxed paper. Chill in refrigerator at least 12 hours.

Slice about ¼ inch thick. Place on cookie sheets and bake at 325 degrees for 10 to 15 minutes, or until light brown. Remove from pans and cool on wire racks.

JAM PASTRIES

Chilling time: 6 *hours or overnight*
Preheat oven to: 400 *degrees*
Utensils needed: At least 2 *ungreased cookie sheets*
Baking time: 10 *to* 15 *minutes. Watch closely*
Quantity: About 5 *dozen*
Storing: Loosely covered container in refrigerator for 1 *week*

¼ *pound chilled margarine*
¼ *pound chilled butter*
½ *pound chilled cream cheese*
2 *cups sifted flour*
jam, jelly, preserves for filling

Cut the margarine, butter and cream cheese into the sifted flour, using your fingertips or a pastry blender. Work into a smooth dough. Form into 1-inch balls. Chill at least 6 hours or overnight. (These may also be frozen before baking.)

When chilled, roll out each ball with the cushion of your hand. Fill center of each with desired filling. Fold sides together and press tight. Bake at 400 degrees for 10 to 15 minutes, or until a pale golden color. Remove from pans and cool on wire racks.

ORANGE COOKIES

Chilling time: 12 *or more hours*
Preheat oven to: 325 *degrees*
Utensils needed: 2 *cookie sheets, greased*
Baking time: 10 *to* 15 *minutes*
Quantity: 8 *dozen*
Storing: Plastic bags tied, for 2 *weeks*

2 *cups shortening*
1 *cup brown sugar*
1 *cup white sugar*
2 *eggs*
5½ *cups sifted flour*
1 *teaspoon salt*
½ *teaspoon baking soda*
4 *tablespoons orange juice*
2 *tablespoons grated orange rind*
1 *cup chopped nuts*

Cream together shortening and sugars until light and fluffy. Add eggs and mix well.

Sift together flour and salt.

Dissolve the baking soda in the orange juice and add alternately with the flour to the creamed shortening-sugar mixture. Blend well. Add grated orange rind and chopped nuts. Mix until blended.

Form dough into long rolls and wrap in waxed paper. Chill in refrigerator at least 12 hours.

Slice about 1/4 inch thick. Place on cookie sheets and bake at 325 degrees for 10 to 15 minutes, or until lightly browned. Remove from pans and cool on wire racks.

COCONUT COOKIES

Chilling time: 12 *hours or more*
Preheat oven to: 325 *degrees*
Utensils needed: 2 *cookie sheets, greased*
Baking time: 10 *to* 15 *minutes*
Quantity: 6 *dozen*
Storing: Plastic bags tied, for 2 *weeks*

2 *cups brown sugar*
2/3 *cup shortening*
2 *eggs, beaten*
1 *teaspoon vanilla*
1 *teaspoon baking soda*
1 *tablespoon hot water*
3 *cups sifted flour*
1 *teaspoon cream of tartar*
1/4 *teaspoon salt*
2 *cups coconut, flaked*

Cream together shortening and sugar until light and fluffy. Add eggs and vanilla. Dissolve baking soda in hot water and add to mixture.

Sift together flour, cream of tartar and salt. Add sifted dry ingredients to shortening-sugar mixture. Blend well. Add coconut and mix until just blended.

Form dough into long rolls and wrap in waxed paper. Chill in refrigerator at least 12 hours.

Slice about 1/4 inch thick. Place on cookie sheets and bake at 325 degrees for 10 to 15 minutes, or until lightly browned. Remove from pans and cool on wire racks.

ITALIAN ANISE COOKIES

Chilling time: 1 *hour*
Preheat oven to: 350 *degrees*
Utensils needed: At least 2 *cookie sheets, greased*
Baking time: 30 *minutes–first time. About* 5 *minutes–second time*
Quantity: About 6 *dozen*
Storing: Airtight container for 4 *weeks. Do not freeze.*

3 *eggs*
1 *cup sugar*
¼ *cup melted butter*
2 *cups sifted flour*
2 *teaspoons baking powder*
1 *teaspoon anise extract*
1 *teaspoon anise seed*
½ *cup chopped almonds*

Beat the eggs and sugar until creamy. Add the melted butter and mix well. Sift the flour and baking powder together into the egg mixture. Beat until well blended and thick. Add the anise extract and seed and the chopped nuts. If the dough seems too soft to roll, add a bit more flour.

Form the dough into rolls about 2 inches thick. Chill in refrigerator about 1 hour. When chilled, bake the whole rolls at 350 degrees for 30 minutes or until quite firm and lightly browned. Remove from oven and slice diagonally on the cookie sheets. Put back in the oven for about 5 minutes. Remove from pans and cool on wire racks.

Cookie-Press Cookies

CHOCOLATE CHEESE COOKIES

Chilling time: 30 *minutes*
Preheat oven to: 375 *degrees*
Utensils needed: At least 2 *ungreased cookie sheets*
Cookie press
Baking time: 8 *to* 10 *minutes*
Quantity: About 5 *dozen*
Storing: Loosely covered container for 1 *week*

1 *cup softened butter*
1 3-*ounce package cream cheese, softened*
1 *cup sugar*
1 *egg*
2 *squares unsweetened chocolate, melted*
2½ *cups sifted flour*
1 *teaspoon baking powder*

Cream together the butter and cream cheese. Add the sugar and beat until light and fluffy. Beat in the egg and melted chocolate. Sift together the flour and baking powder and mix into the creamed mixture. Chill dough for 30 minutes. Pack dough into cookie press and force onto ungreased cookie sheets in desired shapes, 1–1½ inches apart. Bake at 375 degrees for 8 to 10 minutes, or until lightly browned. Remove from pans and cool on wire racks.

LEMON STRIPS

Preheat oven to: 400 *degrees*
Utensils needed: At least 2 *cookie sheets, greased*
Cookie press with pencil-like tip
Baking time: 6 *to* 10 *minutes*
Quantity: About 4 *dozen*
Storing: In layers in tightly covered container for 2 *weeks*

½ cup butter
½ cup sugar
4 egg whites
1 cup sifted flour
1 teaspoon lemon extract
½ teaspoon grated lemon rind

Cream butter until light. Add sugar and continue creaming until fluffy. Add egg whites one at a time and mix well. Stir in the sifted flour, blending all together. Add the lemon extract and rind. Mix into dough.

Place dough in cookie press fitted with pencil-like tip. Press onto prepared baking sheets in 3-to-4-inch strips, at least 1½ inches apart.

Bake at 400 degrees for 6 to 10 minutes, or until lightly browned.

Remove from pans and cool on wire racks.

ORANGE CHEESE COOKIES

Chilling time: At least 15 minutes
Preheat oven to: 400 degrees
Utensils needed: At least 2 ungreased cookie sheets
Cookie press
Baking time: 10 to 12 minutes
Quantity: About 5 dozen
Storing: Airtight in refrigerator for 1 week

½ cup softened butter
1 3-ounce package cream cheese
⅓ cup sugar
1 egg yolk
1½ teaspoons orange extract
1½ cups sifted flour
½ teaspoon salt
1 teaspoon grated orange rind

Cream the butter and cream cheese together until well-blended. Gradually add sugar until mixture is light and fluffy. Add the egg yolk and flavoring; beat well.

Sift flour and salt together. Add to creamed mixture by the half cup, beating well after each addition. Stir in grated orange rind.

Chill at least 15 minutes before using.

Force dough through cookie press directly onto the ungreased cookie sheets, 1–1½ inches apart. Keep unused dough in the refrigerator until you are ready for it. [*cont.*]

Bake at 400 degrees for 10 to 12 minutes, or until lightly browned.

Remove from pans and cool on wire racks.

SCOTCH SHORTBREAD

Preheat oven to: 300 *degrees*
Utensils needed: Cookie press and at least 2 *ungreased cookie sheets or* 2 9-*inch cake pans*
Baking time: Check after 10 *minutes; full time approximately* 20 *minutes*
Quantity: 6 *to* 8 *dozen if made in a cookie press:* 18 1-*inch wedges if made in cake tins*
Storing: Individually plastic-wrapped in loosely covered container for 1 *week; covered and refrigerated for* 2 *weeks*

2 *cups softened sweet butter*
1 *cup sugar*
4⅓ *cups sifted flour*

Cream the butter and sugar together until light and fluffy. Add the flour and mix well.

We prefer to make these cookies in a cookie press. An alternative method, however, is to fit the dough into 2 9-inch cake tins with the edges pressed as for a piecrust. Prick with a fork. Bake at 300 degrees for 10 to 20 minutes, or until lightly browned. When baked, cut the shortbread into pie-shaped slices as soon as it is removed from the oven. Let cool in pans.

If cookies are made in a press, use shapes desired and place on ungreased cookie sheets. Bake at 300 degrees for 10 to 20 minutes, or until edges are lightly browned. Remove from pans and cool on wire racks.

SPRITZ COOKIES

Chilling time: 10 *minutes*
Preheat oven to: 400 *degrees*
Utensils needed: At least 2 *ungreased cookie sheets*
Cookie press

Baking time: 8 *to* 10 *minutes*
Quantity: Approximately 4 *dozen*
Storing: Covered container for 2 *weeks*

1 *cup shortening*
¾ *cup sugar*
1 *egg*
1 *teaspoon lemon extract*
2¼ *cups sifted flour*
½ *teaspoon baking powder*
¼ *teaspoon salt*

Cream shortening and sugar together until light and fluffy. Add egg and lemon extract. Mix well.

Sift together flour, baking powder and salt. Add sifted dry ingredients gradually to shortening-sugar mixture.

Chill dough for 10 minutes. Then pack into cookie press, using shapes desired. Place cookies on ungreased cookie sheets.

Bake at 400 degrees for 8 to 10 minutes, or until lightly browned. Remove from pans and cool on wire racks.

Cutout Cookies

BLACK-WALNUT COOKIES

Preheat oven to: 350 *degrees*
Utensils needed: At least 2 *cookie sheets, greased. Small round cookie cutter dusted with confectioner's sugar*
Baking time: 15 *to* 18 *minutes*
Quantity: About 5 *dozen*
Storing: Airtight container for 10 *days*

1 *cup softened unsalted butter*
¾ *cup superfine sugar*
1 *cup finely ground black walnuts (English walnuts may be substituted)*
2 *cups sifted flour*
confectioner's sugar

Cream the butter until extremely light. Gradually beat in sugar, and mix until fluffy and very pale in color. Stir in the finely ground walnuts, blending well. Gradually sift in flour to make a soft dough.

[*cont.*]

Place dough on a board dusted with either flour or confectioner's sugar. Roll out about ¼ inch thick. Cut into small rounds with prepared cookie cutter. Place on prepared baking sheets at least ½ inch apart.

Bake at 350 degrees for 15 to 18 minutes, or until lightly browned. Cool slightly in pans. Transfer to waxed paper and dust with confectioner's sugar. Finish cooling on wire racks.

OLD-TIME CHRISTMAS CUTOUTS

Standing time: Overnight
Preheat oven to: 350 *degrees*
Utensils needed: At least 2 *cookie sheets, greased*
Cookie cutters or cardboard patterns
Baking time: About 8 *minutes*
Quantity: Hundreds
Storing: Airtight container for 3 *weeks*

3 *cups dark corn syrup*
1 *cup plus* 4 *tablespoons butter*
1½ *cups vegetable shortening*
4 *pounds sifted all-purpose flour*
3 *tablespoons cinnamon*
3 *tablespoons ground cloves*
1 *rounded teaspoon ground cardamom*
2 *tablespoons allspice*
½ *teaspoon ginger*
1 *pound light-brown sugar*
¼ *cup lemon juice*
grated rind of 1 *lemon*
3½ *teaspoons baking soda*
2 *tablespoons warm water*

Place corn syrup, butter and shortening in heavy saucepan over medium heat. Stir until melted. Set aside, but keep warm.

In a very large mixing bowl, mix the flour, spices and sugar. Blend together.

Gradually pour the warm mixture over the flour mixture. Stir by hand. Mix in the lemon juice and rind. Continue mixing and add the soda dissolved in the warm water. Knead dough well.

Let stand at room temperature overnight.

Roll dough paper-thin and cut into shapes. Place on prepared pans and bake at 350 degrees for about 8 minutes, or until lightly browned. Remove from baking pan and cool on wire racks. You may decorate with icing when cooled.

NOTE: These cookies make wonderful Christmas-tree decorations. With a small skewer, pierce a hole about 1/4 inch from the top of each cookie before baking.

VANILLA SNAPS

Chilling time: 1 *hour or more*
Preheat oven to: 350 *degrees*
Utensils needed: Cookie cutters or cardboard patterns. At least 2 *cookie sheets, greased*
Baking time: 12 *to* 15 *minutes*
Quantity: About 4 *dozen, depending on size*
Storing: In layers in loosely covered container for 2 *weeks*

1/3 *cup softened butter*
1 *cup sugar*
1 *egg*
2 *teaspoons pure vanilla extract*
1/4 *cup milk*
2 *cups sifted flour*
small piece vanilla bean, ground
1 1/2 *teaspoons baking powder*
1/4 *teaspoon salt*
confectioner's sugar

Cream butter and sugar until light and fluffy. Add egg and vanilla extract, blending well. Stir in milk. Sift in the flour, ground vanilla bean, baking powder and salt. Mix together to a soft dough.

Chill at least 1 hour.

Place a quarter of the chilled dough at a time on a board or counter top dusted with confectioner's sugar (you can use flour, but you will have a drier cookie). Roll to about 1/8-inch thickness and cut into desired shapes. If you wish to use as tree decorations, make a hole with a small skewer about 1/4 inch from the top of each cookie.

Transfer to prepared cookie sheets and bake at 350 degrees for 12 to 15 minutes, or until lightly browned. Remove from pans and cool on wire racks.

SAND TARTS

Chilling time: 3 *hours*
Preheat oven to: 350 *degrees*
Utensils needed: At least 2 *lightly greased cookie sheets*
Circle cookie cutter
Baking time: 6 *to* 8 *minutes*
Quantity: About 12 *dozen*
Storing: Loosely covered container for 1 *week*

1 *pound unsalted butter*
1 *pound sugar*
2 *eggs*
¼ *pound finely ground almonds*
2 *pounds sifted flour*

Cream the butter and sugar until light and fluffy. Beat in the eggs and finely ground almonds, mixing well. Gradually sift in the flour, stirring by hand until well blended.

Chill dough at least 3 hours.

Roll out about ⅛ inch thick on lightly floured board. Cut into circles and place on prepared cookie sheets. Keep unused dough chilled.

Bake at 350 degrees for 6 to 8 minutes, or until lightly browned. Remove from pans and cool on wire racks.

As a variation, you may brush the tops of unbaked cookies with lightly beaten egg white and sprinkle with cinnamon sugar before baking.

WINE STARS

Chilling time: 3 *hours*
Preheat oven to: 400 *degrees*
Utensils needed: 2 *cookie sheets, lightly greased*
2*-inch star-shaped cookie cutter*
Baking time: 12 *minutes*
Quantity: 6 *dozen*
Storing: Individually plastic-wrapped in loosely covered container for 1 *week*

½ cup soft butter
1⅓ cups brown sugar
1 egg
½ cup finely chopped blanched almonds
3 cups sifted flour
½ teaspoon baking soda
¾ teaspoon cinnamon
2 tablespoons red wine or sherry
⅛ teaspoon almond extract

Cream butter and sugar together until light and fluffy. Beat in egg. Stir in almonds.

Sift together flour, baking soda and cinnamon. Add to butter-sugar mixture along with wine or sherry and flavoring.

Chill 3 hours.

On floured board, roll out ¼ inch thick. Cut into stars with cookie cutter.

Place on prepared cookie sheets and bake at 400 degrees for 12 minutes or until lightly browned. Remove from pans and cool on wire racks.

ICING

Utensils needed: Electric mixer and small mixing bowl. Small bowl for each color
Quantity: About 1½ cups
Do not store.

1½ cups sifted confectioner's sugar
1 egg white
pinch salt
1 teaspoon lemon juice
food coloring

Place all ingredients except food coloring in small mixing bowl. Beat until well blended on medium speed of electric mixer.

If you wish only one icing color, add food coloring drop by drop until you reach shade desired. For a variety of colors, divide the icing as you wish into small bowls. Mix each color individually.

Use as quickly as possible. If icing sets or gets too thick before you are finished decorating, add water a drop at a time.

NOTE: This icing is good for any cookie that calls for trim or decoration.

PART TWO

SWEETS

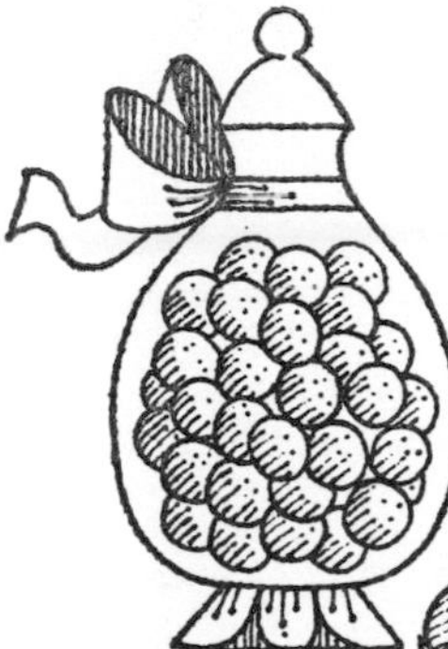

4 · Plum Pudding

Standing time: 1 *hour*
Utensils needed: Large deep steamer or kettle with bottom rack
2 1-*quart molds, well buttered*
Steaming time: 2½ *hours*
Storing: See page 88

1 *cup golden seedless raisins*
½ *cup chopped dried apricots*
½ *cup chopped dates*
1 *cup chopped glazed mixed fruit*
1 *cup apple cider*
1½ *cups firmly packed brown sugar*
4 *eggs*
1 *cup finely minced suet*
½ *cup fine bread crumbs*
½ *cup finely chopped blanched almonds*
½ *cup brandy*
1 *cup sifted flour*
1½ *teaspoons baking powder*
¾ *teaspoon salt*
¾ *teaspoon baking soda*
½ *teaspoon nutmeg*
½ *teaspoon ground cloves*
1 *teaspoon cinnamon*

Place all fruits in bowl. Add the cider and set aside for at least one hour.

In a large mixing bowl, beat the brown sugar and eggs. Add the suet, bread crumbs, nuts and brandy to the sugar and eggs.

Mix well. Add the fruits and cider. Blend well. Sift all dry ingredients into the fruit batter and mix well.

Pour into prepared molds, filling three-quarters full. Cover molds very tightly with a double layer of aluminum foil and tie securely. Place molds on rack, foil up, in a deep steamer. Pour in enough boiling water to cover one half of the molds. Cover steamer tightly. Steam for 2½ hours. Check the water level from time to time and, if necessary, add more water to keep the molds one-half covered at all times. Remove from steamer and immediately remove the secured covers. Cool puddings in their molds on wire racks.

STORING AND FREEZING:

If pudding is to be stored in the molds, re-cover with aluminum foil and tie securely as before. If removed from molds, wrap tightly in double thickness of aluminum foil. Plum pudding will keep at least 4 months under refrigeration. It may be frozen and will keep up to 8 months in freezer.

SERVING:

Plum pudding should be reheated before serving. If frozen, first thaw completely. Then, to reheat, place mold, re-covered with foil and tied as before, in steamer, but steam for only 45 minutes. If out of mold, wrap in foil and place in a heavy pot before setting in steamer. Plum pudding is almost always served with Hard Sauce (See Syrups and Sauces, page 137).

5 · Candy and Nuts

EXCEPT for an occasional batch of fudge, most cooks seem to avoid candy making. As delicious as homemade fudge is, there are many superb varieties of candy to explore. For gift giving, there is nothing more unexpected than homemade candy.

There are two basic methods of preparing candy, thermometer and nonthermometer. Those recipes that do not require a thermometer are usually the easiest and quickest. If you have never tried your hand at candy making, start with an easy recipe (such as Never-Fail Chocolate Fudge). Whichever method you choose, you will find candy making much easier than anticipated, if you follow some basic rules: Always follow the recipe exactly. Do not substitute ingredients until you are a really experienced candy cook. Cook all candy in a heavy saucepan (cast iron is excellent), and use a wooden spoon for stirring.

If you do not own a candy thermometer and are going to make a candy that requires one, we strongly suggest that you purchase one. The cost is not great, and we feel that the investment is well worth it. If this is not possible, keep within reach a small bowl or glass of ice water in which you can test the consistency of the candy. For the ice-water method of testing, use the following descriptions as your guideline:

235–240 *degrees—Soft ball*	*Soft ball is formed when syrup is dropped into water. Ball can be flattened when removed.*
245–248 *degrees—Firm ball*	*As above, except that ball cannot be flattened when removed.*
250–265 *degrees—Hard ball*	*Hard ball, one that holds its shape but can be molded, is formed when syrup is dropped into water.*
270–290 *degrees—Soft crack*	*Hard threads are formed when syrup is dropped into water.*
300–310 *degrees—Hard crack*	*Brittle threads are formed when syrup is dropped into water.*

Gift containers for homemade candy can be of almost any size or shape. One of the easiest is a 1- or 2-pound can with a snap-on plastic lid (coffee, shortening or nut can). Spray-painted and decorated with stick-on decals, the can may be used over and over. Children's shoe boxes; disposable foil pans; boxes for foil, waxed paper or plastic wrap; frozen-food pans and oatmeal containers are a few other ideas for candy holders. They can be decorated with adhesive-backed decorating paper or gift wrap and ribbons. Candy cups can be ordered through a store in our Shopping Guide, or you can make them yourself with small pieces of aluminum foil. They are very helpful packing aids.

Individually wrapped candy pieces can be packed inside a paper tube (such as those on which paper towels are rolled). With a bit of decoration you can make it look like a firecracker or a candle: Seal the bottom with a small piece of cardboard. Make another circular cover to fit the top, and attach to it either a small piece of white string or a piece of yellow ribbon cut into a flame shape. Cover the roll with red paper, glue tightly, and you will have a charming package.

As with other homemade gifts, the dime store and junk shops provide many unusual containers. Apothecary jars, old soda glasses, and antique bowls, boxes or vases make marvelous containers. Fill them with candy, seal with plastic wrap and tie with a bright ribbon bow. Your candy will look almost too good to eat.

We do not suggest shipping candy long distances, unless by airmail. The temperature changes in shipment are sometimes so drastic that the candy either melts or crumbles, however securely wrapped.

Each candy recipe has storing instructions. All candies should be stored in a cool place for maximum life.

Most of our nut recipes are quick and easy. They make particularly good hostess gifts. Nuts are best packed in a can with a snap-on plastic lid. You can purchase these lids (fitting a No. 303-sized can) in most large dime stores or in the housewares departments of department stores. We spray-paint several cans at a time and keep stick-on decals handy so that we are always prepared for gift giving.

Nonthermometer Candy

COCONUT BURSTS

Quantity: 3 *dozen*
Storing: Airtight container for 2 *weeks*

1 8-*ounce package semisweet chocolate squares*
1 *cup flaked coconut*

Heat chocolate squares over hot water until partially melted. Remove from heat and stir until completely melted. Add coconut and mix well. Drop by spoonfuls onto waxed paper and let stand until firm.

BOURBON BALLS

No cooking
Chilling time: 3 *hours*
Setting time: 24 *hours*
Quantity: About 6–7 *dozen*
Storing: Airtight container for 3 *weeks*

2½ *cups crushed vanilla wafers*
1 *cup confectioner's sugar*
2 *tablespoons cocoa*
1 *cup finely chopped walnuts*
¼ *cup bourbon* (*or rum*)
3 *tablespoons white corn syrup*
confectioner's sugar

Place all ingredients in a mixing bowl. Knead together with your hands until well blended.

Roll dough into 1-inch balls. Roll each ball in confectioner's sugar until well coated.

Chill at least 3 hours before storing. Let set at least 24 hours before serving.

PEPPERMINT WAFERS

No cooking
Setting time: 12 *hours*
Quantity: About 1 *pound*
Storing: Loosely covered container for 10 *days. Do not store different flavors together.*

1 *egg white*
2¾ *cups sifted confectioner's sugar*
2 *teaspoons softened unsalted butter*
2 *teaspoons peppermint extract*
few drops red food coloring

Beat the egg white until foamy. Gradually sift in the confectioner's sugar. Mix well. Add the softened butter, extract and food coloring. Blend.

Roll dough into approximately ¾-inch balls. Place on waxed

paper or foil about 1½ inches apart. Flatten with fork tines, making lines go in one direction.

Let set at least overnight before storing.

VARIATIONS:

1. For Wintergreen Wafers: Use 2 teaspoons wintergreen extract and green food coloring.
2. For Spearmint Wafers: Use 2 teaspoons spearmint extract and yellow food coloring.
3. For Fruit-flavored Wafers: Use 2 teaspoons fruit extract (orange, lemon, cherry, etc.) and coloring appropriate to fruit.

PECAN BOURBON CANDY

No cooking
Utensils needed: Cookie sheet covered with waxed paper
Chilling time: 20 *minutes*
Quantity: 2½ *pounds*
Storing: Individually plastic-wrapped in loosely covered container in refrigerator for 1 *week*

¼ *pound butter*
1 *pound confectioner's sugar*
⅓ *cup bourbon*
3 *cups pecan halves*
8 *ounces semisweet chocolate*
1½ *teaspoons butter*

Cream ¼ pound of butter. Add sugar and bourbon alternately, beating until thick and smooth.

Shape mixture into half-teaspoonful-size balls. Press a pecan half on each side of the ball and chill about 20 minutes.

Melt chocolate with 1½ teaspoons of butter. Dip one end of each candy in the chocolate and put on prepared cookie sheet. Chill until firm.

EASY ALMOND BRITTLE

Utensils needed: Double boiler
Baking sheet, buttered
Quantity: 1 *pound*
Storing: Airtight container for 1 *week*

1 6-*ounce package butterscotch pieces*
1 *cup semisweet chocolate pieces*
1 *cup sliced blanched almonds*
salt

Melt butterscotch and chocolate pieces over hot water. Sprinkle almonds lightly with salt and stir into melted candy. Spread out on prepared baking sheet and chill until firm. Then break into pieces.

RAISIN-PEANUT DROPS

Utensils needed: Double boiler
Quantity: About 4 *dozen pieces*
Storing: Layers in tightly covered container for 10 *days*

1 12-*ounce package semisweet chocolate bits*
2 14-*ounce cans sweetened condensed milk*
1 *teaspoon unsalted butter*
2 *cups seedless raisins*
2 *cups chopped unsalted roasted peanuts*

Melt the chocolate bits in top part of double boiler over very hot water. When melted, add the milk and butter. Cook for about 12 minutes, or until mixture is quite thick, stirring constantly. Add the raisins and chopped nuts. Stir until well blended.

Drop by the tablespoonful onto waxed paper or foil. Refrigerate until well set.

NEVER-FAIL CHOCOLATE FUDGE

Utensils needed: Saucepan
Greased flat pan or platter
Boiling time: 6 *minutes*
Quantity: Approximately 65 *pieces*
Storing: Individually plastic-wrapped in airtight container for 1 *week*

- 1 6-*ounce package chocolate bits*
- 1 *teaspoon vanilla*
- ⅛–¼ *pound butter*
- 1 *cup chopped nuts*
- 10 *large-size marshmallows*
- 2 *cups sugar*
- 1 *small can evaporated milk*

Place chocolate bits, vanilla, butter and chopped nuts in a large mixing bowl. Set aside.

Place marshmallows, sugar and evaporated milk in saucepan. Bring to boil over medium heat, stirring constantly. Continue stirring and boil for exactly 6 minutes.

Remove from heat and pour marshmallow mixture over the chocolate mixture in bowl. Beat with a spoon until creamy.

Pour onto prepared pan or platter and cool slightly before cutting into squares.

ALMOND MOUNDS

Preheat oven to: 350 *degrees*
Utensils needed: Double boiler, Baking sheet
Quantity: About 2 *dozen pieces*
Storing: Airtight container for 10 *days*

- 1¼ *cups slivered blanched almonds*
- 1 6-*ounce package semisweet chocolate bits*
- 1 14-*ounce can sweetened condensed milk*
- 1 *teaspoon orange extract*
- 1 *teaspoon grated orange rind*

Place almond slivers on a baking sheet in a 350-degree oven and toast for about 7 minutes. Set aside.

Place chocolate bits and condensed milk in top of double boiler over very hot water (do not boil). Cook, stirring occasionally, for about 20 minutes, or until quite thick. Remove from heat. Stir in extract, rind and toasted almond slivers, blending together well.

Drop by the tablespoon onto waxed paper or foil. Refrigerate until well set.

TURTLES

Utensils needed: Double boiler
Cookie sheets, buttered
Quantity: About 4 *dozen*
Storing: Individually plastic-wrapped in airtight container for 2 *weeks*

1 *pound vanilla caramels*
8 *teaspoons water*
1 *teaspoon vanilla*
1 12-*ounce package semisweet chocolate bits*
2 6-*ounce cans pecan halves*

Melt caramels with water and vanilla over boiling water in double boiler. Cool slightly. Separately, melt chocolate bits and set aside in a warm place.

Place 4 pecan halves on buttered cookie sheet. Spoon about 1 teaspoon of caramel mixture in center of group of nuts, half covering each nut. Repeat until all nuts are used. Let stand about 10 minutes. Spread some melted chocolate over each candy. Let stand until set.

TRUFFLES

Utensils needed: Double-boiler
8-*inch-square pan lined with foil*
Cooling time: 2 *hours*
Quantity: About 2 *pounds*
Storing: Layers in airtight container for 2 *weeks*

1 *egg white*
2 *tablespoons brandy*

2 tablespoons cocoa
1 ½ cups sifted confectioner's sugar
1 ½ cups finely chopped almonds
1 ½ cups grated unsweetened chocolate
¾ cup sweetened condensed milk
1 tablespoon butter

Place the egg white, brandy, cocoa, sifted sugar and almonds in a small bowl. Stir ingredients; then knead together by hand. Form into a layer in the bottom of the prepared pan.

Place the grated chocolate in top of double boiler over hot, but not boiling, water. Melt, stirring occasionally. Add the milk and butter and continue cooking until mixture thickens, about 7 minutes. Pour chocolate mixture over nut mixture in pan. Spread to make an even layer.

Cool at least 2 hours. When cool, cut into approximately 1-inch squares. Let set before storing.

BUTTERSCOTCH NUT DROPS

Utensils needed: Saucepan
Boiling time: 3 minutes
Quantity: 1 ¾ pounds
Storing: Individually plastic-wrapped in airtight container for 2 weeks

2 cups sugar
1 cup light-brown sugar
¾ cup water
¼ cup light corn syrup
1 teaspoon vinegar
½ teaspoon salt
1 6-ounce package butterscotch pieces
1 cup coarsely chopped nuts

Place both sugars, water, corn syrup, vinegar and salt in saucepan. Bring to full boil, stirring constantly. Boil 3 minutes over high heat without stirring. Remove from heat and add butterscotch pieces, stirring until melted. Add nuts and drop by spoonfuls on ungreased tinfoil. If mixture becomes too thick to drop, add a little hot water, a teaspoon at a time. Let stand until set.

DORIS' APPLETS

Utensils needed: Saucepan
8-inch-square pan, greased
Quantity: About 4 dozen pieces
Storing: Individually plastic-wrapped in airtight container for 2 weeks

1 *cup grated Delicious apples*
2 *cups white sugar*
2 *tablespoons unflavored gelatin*
5 *tablespoons cold water*
1 *tablespoon rose extract*
1 *cup finely chopped walnuts*
confectioner's sugar

Place the grated apples and sugar in saucepan over medium heat. Bring to a boil, stirring constantly; boil for one minute. Turn heat low and simmer for 30 minutes.

Soak the gelatin in the water. When apple mixture has finished cooking, dissolve gelatin mixture in it. Stirring constantly, add the extract and nuts.

Pour mixture into prepared pan. Cool at least 2 hours.

Cut into about 1-inch squares and roll each in confectioner's sugar to coat. Let set before wrapping.

ORANGE GUMDROPS

Utensils needed: 2 saucepans
9-inch-square pan, greased
Setting time: 2 hours
Quantity: About 5 dozen
Storing: In layers separated by waxed paper in airtight container for 3 weeks

1 *6-ounce bottle liquid pectin*
¼ *teaspoon baking soda*
¾ *cup sugar*
¾ *cup light corn syrup*
2 *teaspoons orange extract*
1 *teaspoon grated orange rind*
4 *drops yellow food coloring*
2 *drops red food coloring*
granulated sugar

In a small heavy saucepan, stir together the liquid pectin and baking soda. Place the sugar and corn syrup in another heavy saucepan. Set each pan over medium heat. Cook contents of each, stirring frequently, for about 4 minutes, or until foam disappears from pectin mixture.

Pour the pectin mixture into sugar mixture in a slow stream. Bring to a boil; boil for exactly 1 minute. Remove from heat.

Stir in the extract, rind and coloring, and pour at once into prepared pan. Let stand for about 2 hours.

Cut into approximately 1-inch cubes, and roll in granulated sugar until well coated.

Thermometer Candy

HOLIDAY FRUIT CANDY

Utensils needed: Saucepan
Candy thermometer
9-inch loaf pan, greased
Standing time: 12 *hours*
Quantity: 4½ *pounds*
Storing: Individually plastic-wrapped in airtight container for 2 *weeks*

3 *cups sugar*
1 *cup light corn syrup*
1½ *cups heavy cream*
¼ *teaspoon salt*
1 *teaspoon vanilla*
½ *pound pecan halves*
½ *pound walnut halves*
½ *pound almonds*
½ *pound whole candied cherries*
½ *cup diced candied pineapple*

Mix sugar, corn syrup, heavy cream and salt in saucepan. Bring to boil and cook without stirring to 236 degrees on candy thermometer. Remove from heat and let stand 5 minutes.

Add vanilla and beat until slightly thickened. Add nuts and fruits and stir until well mixed and thick.

Pack into prepared pan and let stand overnight or until firm. Turn out of pan and cut into thick slices. Cut each slice into fingers.

JUMBLES

Utensils needed: Saucepan
Candy thermometer
Setting time: 2 hours
Quantity: About 2½ dozen
Storing: Airtight container for 10 days

- ½ *cup white sugar*
- 1 *cup tightly packed light-brown sugar*
- ¼ *cup white corn syrup*
- ½ *cup evaporated milk*
- 2 *tablespoons softened butter*
- 1¼ *cups medium chopped nuts (any kind will do)*
- ½ *cup flaked coconut*
- 1½ *teaspoons maple flavoring*

Place sugars, syrup and milk in saucepan over medium heat. Cook, stirring constantly, until mixture reaches the soft-ball stage (240 degrees on candy thermometer).

Remove from heat. Using a wooden spoon, immediately beat in the butter, nuts, coconut and flavoring. Working quickly, drop mixture by the teaspoonful onto waxed paper or foil. Cool.

Let set at least 2 hours before storing.

PEANUT BRITTLE

Utensils needed: Saucepan
Candy thermometer
2 cookie pans, greased
Setting time: 2 hours
Quantity: About 4 pounds
Storing: Airtight container in layers for 3 weeks

- 1 *cup white corn syrup*
- 4 *cups sugar*
- 5 *cups unsalted roasted peanuts (or other nuts)*
- 1½ *tablespoons butter*
- 2½ *teaspoons baking soda*

Place the syrup and sugar in a saucepan over medium heat. Cook, stirring constantly, until sugar dissolves. Place candy thermometer in pan and continue cooking, without stirring, until syrup reaches soft-ball stage (240 degrees on candy thermometer). Immediately add nuts. Cook, stirring occasionally, until syrup reaches hard-crack stage (300 degrees on candy thermometer).

Remove from heat. Immediately add butter and baking soda, stirring until well blended. Mixture will foam. Quickly pour mixture into prepared pans.

Cool at least 2 hours. Use a knife to break candy into serving pieces. Then let candy set about another 2 hours before storing.

PENUCHE

Utensils needed: Saucepan
Candy thermometer
8-inch-square pan, generously greased
Setting time: 1 *hour*
Quantity: About 2½ *pounds*
Storing: Layers in airtight container for 10 *days*

2 *cups tightly packed light-brown sugar*
1 *cup white sugar*
1 *tablespoon white corn syrup*
¾ *cup milk*
1 *tablespoon butter*
1 *teaspoon vanilla*
1½ *cups chopped walnuts*

Place sugars, syrup, milk and butter in saucepan over medium heat. Cook, stirring constantly, until sugar dissolves. Continue cooking, without stirring, until mixture reaches soft-ball stage (240 degrees on candy thermometer).

Remove from heat. Stir in vanilla and nuts. Beat until mixture is very thick and has begun to lose its gloss. Pour into prepared pan. Let cool at least 1 hour. Cut into approximately 1-inch squares.

COFFEE-BEAN FUDGE

Utensils needed: Saucepan
Candy thermometer
8-inch-square pan, buttered

Quantity: 1½ pounds

Storing: Individually plastic-wrapped in airtight container for 1 week

- 3 cups sugar
- 2 tablespoons instant coffee powder
- ⅛ teaspoon salt
- ½ cup light cream
- 2 tablespoons light corn syrup
- 1 cup milk
- 3 tablespoons butter
- ½ teaspoon rum extract
- coffee beans

Mix sugar, coffee powder, salt, light cream, corn syrup and milk in a saucepan. Bring mixture to boil, stirring constantly. Continue cooking without stirring to 234 degrees on candy thermometer.

Remove from heat. Add butter and rum extract, but do not stir.

Cool to lukewarm. Then beat until mixture begins to thicken and loses its gloss.

Spread in prepared pan. While still warm, mark in squares and press a coffee bean into center of each square. When cold, cut into pieces.

SIMPLE PRALINES

Utensils needed: Saucepan
Candy thermometer

Quantity: About 1 dozen

Storing: Layers in airtight container for 10 days

- 2 cups tightly packed light-brown sugar
- 1 cup light cream
- 1 teaspoon vanilla
- 2½ cups pecan halves

Place sugar and cream in saucepan over medium heat. Cook, stirring constantly, until sugar dissolves. Continue cooking, without stirring, until mixture reaches soft-ball stage (240 degrees on candy thermometer).

Remove from heat. Stir in vanilla. Beat until mixture begins to sugar. Immediately add pecans.

Drop on waxed paper into about 2½-inch patties. Cool before storing.

HARD CANDY

Utensils needed: Saucepan
Candy thermometer
Quantity: About 1 *pound*
Storing: Individually plastic-wrapped in airtight container for 3 *weeks*

2 *cups white sugar*
1 *cup white corn syrup*
½ *cup water*
1 *teaspoon white vinegar*
1½ *teaspoons desired flavoring*
food coloring

Place sugar, syrup, water and vinegar in saucepan over medium heat. Cook, without stirring, until mixture reaches the hard-crack stage (300 degrees on candy thermometer).

Remove from heat and add flavoring and coloring. Mix well. Cool slightly, about 10 minutes, stirring occasionally.

Drop by the teaspoonful onto aluminum-foil sheets, making about 1½-inch circles. If candy hardens before you have finished making circles, return to low heat for a few minutes to melt.

Cool completely before wrapping.

NOTE: You may use half this recipe for small batches of different-flavored hard candies. Fruit, spice and mint flavorings make tasty candies. You may also pour candy into molds made from aluminum foil for Christmas-tree decorations. With a skewer, make a hole about ¼ inch from top of each candy just as it begins to set.

CHOCOLATE NUT CARAMELS

Utensils needed: *Saucepan*
Candy thermometer
8-inch-square pan, greased
Quantity: 1 *pound*
Storing: Individually plastic-wrapped in airtight container for 2 *weeks*

1 15-*ounce can sweetened condensed milk*
1 *cup light corn syrup*
1 *tablespoon butter*
2 *squares unsweetened chocolate*
1 *teaspoon vanilla extract*
¼ *teaspoon rum extract*
⅔ *cup finely chopped nuts*

Mix ⅓ cup condensed milk and corn syrup and butter. Cook over medium heat, stirring constantly, to 235 degrees on candy thermometer. Stir in remaining milk, keeping mixture boiling. Add chocolate, one square at a time. Cook until mixture again reaches 235 degrees on candy thermometer.

Remove from heat and stir in vanilla and rum extracts.

Sprinkle half of nuts in prepared pan and pour in caramel mixture. Sprinkle with remaining nuts and cool thoroughly. Cut into small squares.

CHOCOLATE WALNUT CRUNCH

Utensils needed: *Saucepan*
Candy thermometer
Cookie sheet, greased
Quantity: 2 *pounds*
Cooking time: 45 *minutes*
Storing: Individually plastic-wrapped in airtight container for 1 *week*

1 *pound butter*
2 *cups sugar*
¼ *cup water*
2 *tablespoons light corn syrup*
2 *cups coarsely chopped walnuts*
1 6-*ounce package semisweet chocolate bits*
½ *cup finely chopped walnuts*

Melt butter over low heat. Add sugar and stir until sugar is melted. Add water and corn syrup. Continue cooking without stirring until mixture reaches 290 degrees on candy thermometer.

Remove from heat and stir in coarsely chopped walnuts. Spread in prepared pan and let stand until firm.

Melt chocolate over hot water and spread melted chocolate evenly on candy. Sprinkle with finely chopped walnuts. Let stand until firm and break into pieces.

SESAME BUTTER TOFFEE

Utensils needed: Saucepan
Candy thermometer
Cookie sheet, greased
Preheat oven to: 350 *degrees, to toast sesame seeds*
Cooling time: 2 *hours*
Quantity: About 1½ *pounds*
Storing: Layers in tightly covered container, for 2 *weeks*

1 *cup toasted sesame seeds*
1 *cup melted butter*
1 *cup sugar*
⅓ *cup tightly packed light-brown sugar*
2 *tablespoons water*
¾ *teaspoon baking soda*
3 *squares semisweet chocolate, grated*

To toast sesame seeds: Place on cookie sheet and bake at 350 degrees for about 15 minutes, or until golden brown.

Sprinkle about half the toasted seeds over the bottom of prepared pan. Set other half aside.

Place the melted butter, sugars and water in saucepan. Bring to a boil, stirring constantly. Cook, stirring frequently, to soft-crack stage (290 degrees on candy thermometer). Remove from heat. Immediately stir in baking soda and pour into prepared pan. Cool about 5 minutes.

Sprinkle grated chocolate over top of candy, smoothing as you go. Top with remaining toasted seeds. If necessary, press seeds gently into chocolate. Cool at least 2 hours. Break into serving pieces.

BRANDY ALMOND CHEWS

Utensils needed: Saucepan
Candy thermometer
9-inch-square pan, greased
Boiling time: 5 minutes
Quantity: About 5 dozen
Storing: Individually plastic-wrapped in airtight container for 10 *days*

1 *cup superfine sugar*
1 *cup dark corn syrup*
½ *cup water*
½ *cup light cream*
½ *teaspoon salt*
4 *teaspoons butter*
4 *squares unsweetened chocolate*
2 *teaspoons brandy*
1 *cup unblanched toasted whole almonds*

In saucepan mix sugar, corn syrup, water, light cream and salt. Bring to boil and boil 5 minutes. Add the butter and cook gently, stirring occasionally, to 230 degrees on candy thermometer. Add chocolate, bring to boil again and cook, stirring occasionally, until candy thermometer registers 240 degrees. Remove from heat and stir in brandy. Pour into prepared pan. Cool completely.

When candy is cool, lift whole piece from pan and cut into squares. Put 2 almonds in center of each square. With your fingers, shape the candy into an oblong, covering the nuts.

DIVINITY

Utensils needed: Saucepan
Candy thermometer
Electric mixer
9-inch-square pan, greased
Setting time: 2 hours
Quantity: About 1¾ *pounds*
Storing: Layers in tightly covered container for 1 *week*

3 *cups sugar* (*white* or *light brown*)
½ *cup white corn syrup*
¼ *teaspoon salt*
⅔ *cup warm water*
2 *egg whites*
1 *teaspoon vanilla* (*or other flavoring*)
1 *cup chopped nuts* (*optional*)

Place sugar, syrup, salt and water in saucepan over medium heat. Cook, stirring constantly, until sugar dissolves. Continue cooking, without stirring, until mixture reaches the firm-ball stage (248 degrees on candy thermometer).

Stiffly beat the egg whites. Very slowly, pour about half the syrup mixture over them, mixing constantly.

Continue cooking the other half of the syrup mixture until it reaches the soft-crack stage (270 degrees on candy thermometer). Add it slowly to the egg white/syrup mixture. Beat until it is thick and creamy and holds its shape. Add flavoring and nuts (if desired).

Spread in prepared pan or drop by the teaspoonful onto waxed paper. If placed in pan, let set at least 2 hours before cutting into squares.

NOTE: If desired, you can add ½ cup chocolate bits or ½ cup candied fruit to this recipe in place of the nuts.

POPCORN BALLS

Utensils needed: Saucepan
Candy thermometer
Large bowl, greased
Quantity: About 1 *dozen medium balls*
Storing: Each ball in tightly closed plastic wrap, in dry place up to 2 *weeks*

1 *cup sugar*
⅓ *cup white corn syrup*
1 *cup water*
¼ *teaspoon salt*
1 *teaspoon lemon extract*
food coloring (*optional*)
3 *quarts popped corn*
margarine to grease hands

Place sugar, syrup and water in saucepan over medium heat. Cook, stirring frequently, to the medium-crack stage (280 degrees on candy thermometer). Remove from heat. Immediately add salt, extract and food coloring (if desired). Mix well.

Quickly pour syrup over popped corn in a large greased bowl. Stir with a fork, making sure most pieces of corn are coated. Working fast, grease your hands and scoop up enough coated corn to make a medium-sized ball. Shape and place on waxed paper to cool. This must be done very quickly or the syrup will cool and it will be impossible to form balls. Cool thoroughly before storing.

Popcorn balls in red and green make marvelous Christmas-tree ornaments. String them with a needle and heavy thread.

Nut Candies

SUGARED NUTS

Utensils needed: Saucepan
Candy thermometer
Pie pan
Quantity: 1½ *pounds*
Storing: Airtight container for 2 *weeks*

1 *cup sugar*
2 *cups maple syrup*
1½ *pounds walnut or pecan halves*
granulated sugar for coating
confectioner's sugar for dusting

Combine 1 cup sugar and maple syrup in saucepan. Bring to a boil and boil gently to 230 degrees on candy thermometer. Remove from heat and cool slightly.

Spread a layer of nuts in bottom of pie pan. Dribble syrup over nuts, stirring with a metal spoon. Add more nuts and repeat process until all nuts are coated with syrup.

Place granulated sugar on large pan or platter. With a slotted spoon, lift nuts out of the syrup. Place on sugar and stir until well coated. Dust with confectioner's sugar. Dry thoroughly before storing.

CHOCOLATE-DIPPED ALMONDS

Preheat oven to: 300 *degrees*
Utensils needed: Cookie sheet
Double boiler
Baking time: 10 *to* 15 *minutes*
Storing: Airtight container for 2 *weeks*

Whole, unblanched almonds (as many pounds as you wish to prepare)
1 *or more packages semisweet chocolate bits*

Blanch almonds and toast in slow oven, 300 degrees, for 10 to 15 minutes, or until golden brown. Cool.

Melt chocolate bits over hot water in double boiler. Dip one end of each almond into the chocolate mixture. Put on waxed paper on a platter and chill until chocolate is firm.

ORANGE WALNUTS

Utensils needed: Saucepan
Candy thermometer
Quantity: 2½ *cups*
Storing: Airtight container for 2 *weeks*

¼ *cup lukewarm water*
3½ *tablespoons orange juice*
1 *tablespoon white corn syrup*
1½ *cups sugar*
¼ *cup grated orange rind*
1 *teaspoon grated lemon rind*
2½ *cups walnut halves*

Place water, orange juice, syrup and sugar in saucepan over medium heat. Cook, stirring constantly, until mixture begins to boil. Continue to cook, without stirring, until mixture reaches the soft-ball stage (240 degrees on candy thermometer).

Remove from heat. Immediately add the grated rinds and walnut halves. Stir gently until mixture is creamy and nuts are well coated. Turn out onto a large sheet of waxed paper or foil. Separate nuts with 2 forks. Cool thoroughly before storing.

MINTED WALNUTS

Utensils needed: Saucepan
Candy thermometer
Quantity: About 1¼ pounds
Storing: Airtight container for 3 weeks

1 *cup sugar*
¼ *cup light corn syrup*
½ *cup water*
1¼ *teaspoons peppermint extract*
10 *large marshmallows*
3 *cups walnut halves*

Place sugar, syrup and water in saucepan over medium heat. Cook, stirring constantly, until mixture begins to boil. Continue to cook, without stirring, until mixture reaches the soft-ball stage (240 degrees on candy thermometer).

Remove from heat. Immediately stir in the peppermint extract and marshmallows. Stir until marshmallows are dissolved. Quickly add the walnut halves. Stir until all nuts are well coated.

Pour nuts onto a large sheet of waxed paper or foil. Separate nuts with 2 forks. Cool well before storing.

GLAZED NUTS

Utensils needed: Saucepan
Candy thermometer
Quantity: 1 *pound*
Storing: Airtight container up to 2 *weeks*

1½ *cups sugar*
½ *cup honey*
½ *cup water*
½ *teaspoon vanilla*
1 *pound nuts* (*walnuts, almonds, pecans, Brazil nuts—any one kind or a combination*)

Mix sugar, honey and water in a saucepan. Bring to boil and cook without stirring to 242 degrees on a candy thermometer.

Remove from heat and stir in nuts and vanilla. Let cool slightly.

Stir again until creamy. Then place on waxed paper and separate nuts with 2 forks.

SOUR-CREAM CANDIED NUTS

Utensils needed: Saucepan
Candy thermometer
Quantity: About 1 pound
Storing: Individually plastic-wrapped in airtight container for 2 weeks

1½ *cups sugar*	1 *teaspoon vanilla*
½ *cup sour cream*	2½ *cups walnut halves*

Mix sugar and sour cream in saucepan. Bring to a boil and cook, stirring, until 236 degrees is reached on candy thermometer.

Remove from heat and add vanilla. Beat until mixture thickens and loses its gloss. Add nuts and stir to coat them on all sides. Put on greased cookie sheet and separate nuts.

SPICED MIXED NUTS

Preheat oven to: 350 degrees
Utensils needed: Cookie sheet
Baking time: 15 minutes
Quantity: 2½ cups
Storing: Airtight container for 4 weeks

¼ *cup vegetable oil*	½ *teaspoon nutmeg*
2 *cups sifted confectioner's sugar*	½ *teaspoon cinnamon*
	1½ *teaspoons brandy*
1 *egg white, slightly beaten*	1½ *cups unsalted mixed nuts*

Cream together all ingredients except nuts. Put nuts on cookie sheet and heat in 350-degree oven for 15 minutes. Add to creamed spice-oil mixture and stir well to coat each nut. Spread out on cooled cookie sheet or platter to dry. Separate nuts when cooled.

6 · Jellies, Jams, Marmalades, Conserves, Tutti-Frutti

HOMEMADE jellies, jams, marmalades and conserves are easy to make. In almost all of the recipes that follow we have used commercial fruit pectin. This ensures that your product will turn out correctly. For any recipe using commercial pectin, you should always use fully ripe fruit.

For making the recipes in this chapter, the following utensils are required:

Large *heavy* kettle for cooking the fruit.

Large kettle or pot for boiling jars and covers; or you may use a large roasting pan.

One-pound empty coffee can for melting paraffin.

Wire rack for cooling jars.

Tongs for lifting jars out of sterilizing bath.

Large metal spoon for skimming.

Large wooden spoon for stirring.

You do not have to use proper jelly or jam jars. Any mayonnaise, instant-coffee, baby-food or spaghetti-sauce jars you have in your cupboard will do as well. Be sure that they are thoroughly scoured and rinsed and are odorless before use.

All of the following recipes are to be cooked in an uncovered kettle.

If you do purchase jars, we find that the jelly jars with loose-fitting metal lids are best. These hold about 8 ounces. There are also canning jars in various sizes. We prefer the type with a two-part cover: an inner rim lined with rubber and an outer cap which screws on over it. We think that the 8-ounce size is best for this type of jar also. It is not necessary to seal these with paraffin before putting the lids on. Sterilize lids and jars together, and screw on tops immediately after filling.

Paraffin for sealing jars can be bought in almost any hardware store or supermarket. *Always* place paraffin in a separate container, preferably a coffee can, and *set it in a pan filled with water*. Heat the water over medium heat, being careful that it does not bubble over into the paraffin. It is important to remember *never to melt paraffin over direct heat; it is highly flammable*. If paraffin hardens before you are ready to use it, just reheat it to melt again.

Jars and lids to be sterilized must first be washed and rinsed. Then place them in a large kettle (or roasting pan) with enough water to cover. Bring them to a boil slowly and simmer for about 20 minutes, uncovered. When jam is ready, remove jars from water with a pair of tongs and place on wire racks. *Immediately* fill jars with *hot* jam to within ½ inch of the top. If jelly jars are used, seal immediately with ⅛-inch layer of hot paraffin. When paraffin has hardened completely, cover with an additional ⅛-inch layer of melted paraffin. After this layer hardens completely, cover with lids. If you do not have jar lids, a double piece of aluminum foil held by a rubber band will be sufficient.

If you are using canning jars with screw-top covers, tighten again after jars have cooled completely.

You can decorate just the lid or the entire jar. Lids may be covered with foil, felt, crepe paper or adhesive-backed decorating paper. Bows or small ornaments may be attached with double-faced masking tape. A very simple method of decoration is to buy notary seals and cover the tops with them.

For those of you with a bit more patience, you can wind raffia or colored yarn around the tops. To do this, thinly spread lids with white glue. Start at the edge of the rim and carefully wind raffia or yarn around, keeping rows very close together. Reapply a small amount of glue if necessary. Apply small amount of glue to the end of the raffia or yarn and tuck it under, using a clean toothpick.

You can also decorate tops simply by gluing peppercorns, popcorn (unpopped), beans, poppy seeds and cloves in a pattern on jar lids. You do not have to use all of these, but a combination is most attractive. The lids should then be sprayed with clear plastic to preserve the design.

The jars themselves may be decorated with china markers in whatever design you wish. You may also make stripes with colored plastic tape or cut designs out of self-adhesive plastic. The decorated jars can then be placed in homemade drawstring bags or small foil or gift bags of the correct size.

Homemade jellies, jams, marmalades and conserves store indefinitely in the pantry exactly like store-bought ones.

Jellies

MINT JELLY

Utensils needed: Kettle
Cheesecloth bag
Boiling time: 1 *minute*
Quantity: About 4 *4-ounce jars*

2 *fresh mint leaves per jar*
2 *cups bottled apple juice*
3½ *cups sugar*
1 *teaspoon dried mint, tied in a cheesecloth bag*
½ *bottle liquid pectin*

Wash mint leaves carefully. Set aside.

Mix apple juice, sugar and dried mint (in bag) in kettle. Place over high heat and bring quickly to a boil, stirring constantly. When mixture starts to boil, immediately add liquid pectin. Bring to a full rolling boil. Boil, stirring constantly, for exactly 1 minute.

Remove from heat. Skim off foam with a metal spoon and discard bag of dried mint. Put 2 fresh mint leaves in each hot, sterilized jar. Immediately pour in jelly. Seal with paraffin as directed on page 113. When cool, cover with lids.

SPICY GRAPE JELLY

Utensils needed: Kettle
Cheesecloth bag
Boiling time: 1 *minute*
Quantity: About 5 4-*ounce jars*

1 *pint bottled unsweetened grape juice*
2 *cups cold water*
2 *drops white vinegar*
4 *whole allspice*
3 *large cinnamon sticks, broken*
15 *whole cloves*
1 *box powdered pectin*
3½ *cups sugar*

Place juice and water in kettle. Stir and add vinegar. Tie all spices together in cheesecloth bag and add to juice mixture. Stir in powdered pectin.

Place kettle over high heat. Stirring frequently, bring to a full, rolling boil and immediately add sugar. Bring again to a full, rolling boil. Stir and boil for 1 minute. Remove from heat and skim off foam with a metal spoon. Remove spice bag and pour jelly into hot, sterilized jars. Seal with paraffin.

NOTE: When giving this jelly as a gift, let recipient know that although it is tasty on toast, it is particularly good with meats or as a glaze.

CRANBERRY-CLARET JELLY

Utensils needed: Double boiler
Quantity: 4 4-*ounce jars*

3½ *cups sugar*
1 *cup bottled cranberry juice*
1 *cup claret wine*
½ *bottle fruit pectin*

Put sugar, cranberry juice and wine in top of double boiler and mix well. Place over rapidly boiling water and stir until sugar is dissolved, about 2 minutes. Remove from heat and stir in bottled fruit pectin. Skim off foam and pour at once into 4 sterilized jars. Cover with paraffin.

ROSÉ-WINE JELLY

Utensils needed: Kettle
Quantity: About 4 *4-ounce jars*

2 *cups rosé wine*
⅛ *teaspoon lemon juice*
2 *tablespoons powdered pectin*
3 *cups sugar*
5 *or more whole cloves per jar*

Place wine, lemon juice and powdered pectin in kettle over high heat. Cook, stirring constantly, to the simmering point. Immediately add sugar. Cook, stirring constantly, until jelly comes to a full, rolling boil. Quickly remove from heat and skim off foam with a metal spoon.

Place at least five cloves in the bottom of each hot, sterilized jar. Pour in jelly. If desired, you can at this point also add a mint leaf. Seal with paraffin.

Let jelly set about 1 hour; then turn jars upside down and shake gently to distribute cloves.

NOTE: When giving as gift, let recipient know that this jelly is used primarily as a glaze for or accompaniment to meats.

MARJORAM OR SAGE JELLY

Utensils needed: Kettle
Cheesecloth
Standing time: 20 *minutes*
Quantity: 4 *4-ounce jars*

1 *cup boiling water*
2 *tablespoons dried marjoram* or *dried sage*
⅓ *cup lemon juice*
3 *cups sugar*
½ *cup bottled fruit pectin*
2 *to* 3 *drops food coloring—red for marjoram, green for sage*

Pour boiling water over marjoram or sage. Cover and let stand 20 minutes. Strain through cheesecloth and add enough water to make 1 cup. Strain lemon juice through cheesecloth. Place herb infusion and lemon juice in kettle over high heat and add sugar. Stir well and bring to boil. Add pectin and stir vigorously. Add food coloring and continue stirring until mixture comes to full, rolling boil. Boil hard for exactly ½ minute. Remove from heat and skim with metal spoon. Pour at once into hot, sterilized jars and seal with paraffin.

NOTE: These jellies are served primarily with meats or poultry. They are both good with chicken, veal, ham or roast beef.

Jams

APPLE BUTTER

Utensils needed: Kettle
Strainer
Quantity: About 10 8-*ounce jars*

8 *pounds apples*
4 *cups apple cider*
½ *cup sugar for each cup of cooked fruit*
4 *teaspoons cinnamon*
2 *teaspoons ground cloves*
1 *teaspoon allspice*
grated lemon rind and juice (optional)

Wash, stem and quarter apples. Place cider in kettle. Add apples and cook slowly until soft.

Put the fruit through a fine strainer to remove seeds and skins. Measure fruit, and for each cup of fruit add ½ cup sugar. Mix well. Add spices. Add lemon rind and juice if desired.

Cook slowly over low heat, stirring until sugar is dissolved. Then cook rapidly until butter is thick enough. To test for thickness, chill a saucer in refrigerator and place a spoonful of butter on cold saucer. If no rim of liquid separates from butter, it is thick enough.

Pour into hot, sterilized jars and seal with paraffin.

MOM'S STRAWBERRY JAM

Utensils needed: Kettle
Preparation time: Allow 3 days
Quantity: According to quantity of berries used

Strawberries
Sugar—1 *pound to each pound of berries*

Wash and hull berries and place in kettle. Pour sugar over them. Cover. Set aside for 24 hours in a cool place. Do not refrigerate.

Place kettle over medium heat and bring fruit and sugar to a boil. Boil, without stirring, for 5 minutes. Remove from heat. Cover. Set aside for 24 hours in a cool place.

Pour preserves (these are put up cool; do not reheat them) into hot, sterilized jars. Seal with paraffin.

FOUR-FRUIT JAM

Utensils needed: Kettle
Cooking time: Until jam thickens
Quantity: About 10 8-*ounce jars*

1 *quart strawberries*
1 *quart ripe currants*
1 *quart red raspberries*
1 *quart red cherries*
water
4½ *pounds sugar*

Wash, stem and pit fruit and place in kettle. Add enough water so that you can see it in the fruit, but not enough to cover fruit. Stir in the sugar.

Place kettle over high heat, stirring constantly until mixture boils. Reduce heat to medium and continue cooking, stirring occasionally, until jam begins to thicken.

Pour into hot, sterilized jars and seal with paraffin.

RASPBERRY-APPLE JAM

Utensils needed: Kettle
Quantity: About 7 8-*ounce jars*

6 *cups sugar*
2 *cups water*
2 *pounds cooking apples, grated*
1 *quart red raspberries*

Place sugar and water in kettle over medium heat. Bring to a boil and boil for 15 minutes.

Peel apples and grate them (or chop very fine). Add to the boiling syrup. Stir for about 2 minutes. Add raspberries. Bring to a boil and boil for 9 minutes.

Remove from heat. Pour into hot, sterilized jars. Cover with melted paraffin.

BLUEBERRY JAM

Utensils needed: Kettle
Quantity: About 12 8-*ounce jars*

4½ *cups crushed blueberries* (*about* 1½ quarts whole)
2 *tablespoons lemon juice*
7 *cups sugar*
1 *bottle fruit pectin*

Crush berries thoroughly. Measure 4½ cups into kettle. Add lemon juice. Add sugar and mix well. Place over high heat and bring to full, rolling boil. Boil hard 1 minute, stirring constantly.

Remove from heat and add fruit pectin. Stir and skim off foam for 5 minutes.

Ladle immediately into hot, sterilized jars and seal at once with paraffin.

PEACH OR PEAR JAM

Utensils needed: Kettle
Quantity: 11 *8-ounce jars*

- 4 *cups chopped fruit (about* 3 *pounds)*
- ¼ *cup lemon juice*
- 7½ *cups sugar*
- ½ *bottle fruit pectin*

Peel and pit or core fruit. Chop very fine. Measure 4 cups fruit into kettle. Add lemon juice, then exact amount of sugar. Mix well.

Place over high heat and bring to full rolling boil. Boil hard for 1 minute, stirring constantly.

Remove from heat and stir in fruit pectin. Skim and stir for 5 minutes.

Cool slightly; then ladle at once into hot, sterilized jars and seal with paraffin.

SOUR-CHERRY JAM

Utensils needed: Kettle
Quantity: Approximately 11 8-*ounce jars*

- 3 *pounds fully ripe sour cherries, stemmed and pitted*
- 7 *cups sugar*
- 1 *bottle commercial pectin*
- ¼ *to* ½ *teaspoon almond extract*
- ¼ *cup finely chopped almonds*

Chop cherries into fine pieces to make 4 cups. Put into kettle. Add sugar and mix well.

Bring to a full, rolling boil over high heat and boil hard for 1 minute, stirring constantly.

Remove from heat and immediately stir in pectin. Skim foam off the top with a metal spoon, stirring and skimming for 5 minutes.

Add enough almond extract to produce a very distinctive

cherry taste. Add chopped almonds. Ladle into hot, sterilized jars and seal at once with paraffin.

Marmalades

APPLE MARMALADE

Utensils needed: Kettle
Cooking time: About 30 *minutes*
Quantity: About 3 8-*ounce jars*

1 *large clean-skinned orange*
1 *large clean-skinned lemon*
3 *tablespoons lemon juice*
¾ *cup water*
2 *cups sugar*
1 *large jar chunky apples & apricots*
1 *teaspoon cinnamon*

Seed the orange and slice into very thin strips, being careful not to lose juice. Peel the lemon, cutting only the colored part of the rind. Slice into very thin strips. Squeeze the lemon for its juice. Measure 3 tablespoons (you may need an extra lemon) and set juice aside.

Place the water and sugar in kettle over medium heat. Cook, stirring constantly, until sugar is dissolved. Add the orange and lemon-peel strips. Simmer 15 minutes, stirring frequently. Add apple/apricot mixture and cinnamon. Raise heat and, stirring constantly, bring to a full rolling boil. Lower heat and simmer for 15 minutes, stirring constantly.

Remove from heat. Stir in the lemon juice. Immediately pour into hot, sterilized jars. Seal with paraffin.

ORANGE OR LIME MARMALADE

Utensils needed: Food grinder (optional)
Kettle
Preparation time: Allow 3 days
Quantity: About 5 8-ounce jars

3 *large clear oranges*	OR	9 *large limes*
3 *large lemons*		1 *large lemon*
water		*water*
sugar		*sugar*

Wash fruit. Cut in half and seed. Either grind fruit on medium blade of food grinder or slice very, very thin. Do not lose juice.

Measure the ground fruit. To each cup fruit add 3 cups water. Mix thoroughly. Place in kettle and let stand 24 hours, covered, in a cool place. Do not refrigerate.

Place over medium heat and cook, stirring constantly, until mixture comes to a boil. Boil, without stirring, for 10 minutes. Again, set aside as above.

Measure the cooked fruit. Add 1 cup more sugar than fruit. Cook over medium heat, stirring frequently, for about 30 minutes, or until marmalade begins to jell. Pour immediately into hot, sterilized jars and seal with paraffin.

APRICOT-ORANGE-PINEAPPLE MARMALADE

Utensils needed: Kettle
Cooking time: About 45 minutes
Quantity: About 10 8-ounce jars

1 *large fresh pineapple*
3 *pounds fresh apricots*
1 *large clear-skinned orange*
¾ *cup sugar to each cup fruit*
½ *teaspoon ginger*

Peel, core and cube pineapple. Pit and quarter apricots. Seed and chop orange. Do not lose juice from fruits. Combine the fruit and measure as you pour into heavy kettle. Add ¾ cup sugar for each cup fruit. Stir in the ginger.

Cook over medium heat for about 45 minutes, or until marmalade is thick and clear. Pour into hot, sterilized jars and seal with paraffin.

NOTE: You may use canned crushed pineapple (1 1-pound-4-ounce can) and dried apricots (1 pound, soaked in water overnight), using the water and juice from both. You will, however, lose the marvelous fresh taste. If you are using dried apricots, try to purchase those not preserved with sulfur dioxide.

HONEY-GRAPEFRUIT MARMALADE

Utensils needed: Food grinder
Kettle
Preparation time: Allow 4 *days*
Quantity: About 8 8-*ounce jars*

1 *large clean-skinned grapefruit*
1 *large lemon*
water
half as much sugar as cooked fruit
half as much honey as cooked fruit

Peel the grapefruit and lemon, cutting only the colored part of the rind. Slice the peel into very thin strips.

Seed the pulp. Put the pulp, including the white of the rind, through the coarsest blade of food grinder. Do not lose juice.

Place the rind and pulp in kettle, measuring as you go. For each cup fruit, add 3 cups cold water. Let set, tightly covered, for 24 hours.

Place over medium heat and cook, stirring frequently, until mixture comes to a boil. Boil for 15 minutes. Cover and let stand 24 hours.

Again, cook as above. Cover and let stand another 24 hours.

Remeasure mixture. Add half as much sugar and half as much honey. Cook, stirring frequently, until mixture is thick and clear and has begun to jell. Pour into hot, sterilized jars and seal with paraffin.

Conserves

GRAPE CONSERVE

Utensils needed: *Kettle*
Sieve
Cooking time: About 30 *minutes*
Quantity: About 12 8-*ounce jars*

4 *cups Concord grapes*
¼ *cup lemon juice*
1 *tablespoon grated lemon rind*
½ *cup seedless raisins*
1 *cup finely chopped walnuts*
7 *cups sugar*
½ *bottle liquid pectin*

Slip skins from grapes. Bring pulp to a boil and simmer, covered, 5 minutes.

Put cooked grapes through a sieve. Chop the skins and add to pulp. Measure 4 cups fruit into kettle. Add juice, rind, raisins and nuts.

Add sugar to fruit and mix well. Place over high heat, bring to a full boil and boil hard for 1 minute, stirring constantly. Remove from heat and stir in pectin.

Skim off foam with a large metal spoon. Pour at once into hot, sterilized jars. Seal with paraffin.

PLUM CONSERVE

Utensils needed: Food grinder
Kettle
Cooking time: About 45 *minutes*
Quantity: About 6 8-*ounce jars*

4 *pounds plums*
2 *clear-skinned oranges*
1 *cup tightly packed seedless white raisins*
juice of 1 *lemon*
¾ *cup sugar to each cup ground fruit*
1 *pound walnuts, chopped*

Wash and pit the plums. Wash, seed and quarter oranges.

Put the plums, oranges and raisins through the medium blade of a food grinder. Do not lose juice. Add lemon juice to fruit. Measure ground fruit and add ¾ cup sugar to each cup fruit.

Place in a kettle and simmer over medium heat, stirring frequently, for about 45 minutes, or until mixture begins to thicken.

Remove from heat. Stir in chopped nuts and immediately pour into hot, sterilized jars. Seal with paraffin.

APRICOT CONSERVE

Utensils needed: Kettle
Preparation time: Allow 2 days
Quantity: About 5 8-ounce jars

1 *pound dried apricots*
1 *quart cold water*
1 *orange*
juice of 1 *orange*
juice of 1 *lemon*
1 *cup seedless white raisins*
½ *teaspoon almond extract*
1 *pound sugar*
1 *pound chopped almonds*

Place apricots in kettle and cover with 1 quart cold water. Cover tightly and let stand 24 hours.

Seed and chop the orange. Add the chopped orange, juices, raisins, extract and sugar to the apricots and water. Cook over medium heat, stirring constantly, until mixture comes to the boiling point. Boil, stirring occasionally, until conserve is thick and clear. Quickly stir in chopped nuts.

Remove from heat and pour into hot, sterilized jars. Seal with paraffin.

CRANBERRY CONSERVE

Utensils needed: Kettle
Cooking time: About 15 *minutes*
Quantity: 4 8-*ounce jars*

2 *cups water*
2 *cups sugar*
1 *pound cranberries*
grated rind of 1 *orange*
½ *cup broken walnuts*
2 *teaspoons crystallized ginger*

Place water and sugar in kettle and stir until sugar is dissolved. Boil for 5 minutes, then add cranberries. Simmer until the skins pop on berries and mixture is thick and clear. This should take about 10 minutes.

Add grated orange rind, walnuts and ginger. Immediately pour into hot, sterilized jars and seal with paraffin.

SPICED RHUBARB CONSERVE

Utensils needed: Kettle
Cooking time: 45 *minutes to* 1 *hour*
Quantity: About 6 8-*ounce jars*

4 *cups diced rhubarb*
2 *lemons*
2 *oranges*
1 *cup seedless raisins*
1 *teaspoon cinnamon*
4 *cups sugar*
1½ *cups chopped walnuts*

Place diced rhubarb in kettle.

Seed and juice the lemons and oranges. Remove the pulp and discard it. Slice the skin very fine and add the juice and rind to the rhubarb. Stir in the raisins, cinnamon and sugar.

Cook over medium heat, stirring constantly, until sugar is dissolved. Bring to a boil. Boil gently, without stirring, about 45 minutes, or until mixture is thick and clear.

Remove from heat. Stir in chopped nuts. Pour into hot, sterilized jars. Seal with paraffin.

TUTTI-FRUTTI

Utensils needed: Stone crock—capacity at least 8 *quarts*
No cooking
Preparation time: Allow 5 *to* 6 *weeks*
Quantity: About 14 8-*ounce jars*

1 *pound peaches*
1 *pound plums*
1 *pound pears*
1 *pound nectarines*
1 *pound green grapes*
1 *pound red grapes*
1 *pound black grapes*
7 *pounds sugar*

Prick the peaches, plums, pears and nectarines with a fork. Pack all the fruit into the crock in layers, covering each fruit layer with sugar. Cover and let stand in a cool place, stirring up every three days.

After one week, when the fruit floats, press down with a plate and nonmetal weight and cover with waxed paper. Let fruit stand, stirring occasionally, until fermentation is complete—about one month or so.

When fermentation is complete, pack into sterilized jars and seal.

NOTE: Tutti-Frutti may be used as a dessert, or the fruit may be glazed in roasting-pan juices and served with duck, poultry or pork. We suggest that you give these serving directions along with your gift.

7 · Syrups, Sauces and Flavors

SYRUPS, SAUCES and flavors are among the easiest of gifts in this book.

Syrups can be used to make refreshing summer drinks or as an additive to punches. They are wonderful on waffles, pancakes, French toast or ice cream.

Three different dessert sauces, we think, make a lovely house gift. They can be made quickly and are always handy. They enable the recipient to turn plain cake or ice cream into a festive treat.

You can give the flavored or spiced sugar with a tin of imported cocoa or a fine tea. The flavored coconut is a great extra with dessert sauces; or for someone who likes to bake, it is an excellent addition to any cake.

We recommend using 12-ounce bottles (such as those from ketchup, carbonated beverages or maple syrup) for our syrups. For most of the sauces, we recommend the use of smaller (4-ounce) jars. The flavors do best in a small mustard-type jar. Empty spice jars are also good for the flavors, but do be sure that they are odorless before use. All bottles and jars used must have tight-fitting caps.

For those recipes in this chapter whose containers need sterilizing and sealing, please follow the instructions given in Chapter 6, page 113.

Syrups

CINNAMON SYRUP

Utensils needed: Heavy saucepan
Cooking time: About 45 minutes
Quantity: 1 12-ounce bottle
Storing: Airtight container, refrigerated, up to 6 weeks

4 *cups apple juice*
1 *cup light corn syrup*
½ *cup red-hot cinnamon candies*
1 *stick cinnamon*

Combine all ingredients in saucepan over medium heat. Bring to a boil, lower heat and simmer until syrup is reduced to about 2½ cups; this should take about 45 minutes.

Pour, including the cinnamon stick, into sterilized 12-ounce bottle. Cap tightly and refrigerate.

APRICOT SYRUP

Utensils needed: Heavy saucepan
Electric blender
Cooking time: About 30 minutes
Quantity: 2 12-ounce bottles
Storing: Airtight containers, refrigerated, up to 6 weeks

1 11-*ounce box dried apricots*
water
1 *cup dark corn syrup*
1 *cup light corn syrup*
juice of 1 *lemon*
juice of 1 *orange*

Place apricots in saucepan and cover with water. Place over medium heat and simmer, covered, until tender—about 20 minutes. Drain, reserving about 1 cup apricot cooking water.

Put the apricots in container of electric blender. Puree at high speed, adding apricot cooking liquid as necessary, for just a few seconds.

[*cont.*]

Pour pureed apricots back into the saucepan and add all remaining ingredients. Bring to a boil, lower heat and simmer for 10 minutes. If syrup is too thick add up to ½ cup cold water.

Pour into sterilized bottles. Cap tightly and refrigerate.

APPLE SYRUP

Utensils needed: Heavy saucepan
Cooking time: About 15 *minutes*
Quantity: 1 12-*ounce bottle*
Storing: Airtight container, refrigerated, up to 6 *weeks*

1 *cup apple juice*
2 *cups sugar*
1 *cinnamon stick*

Combine all ingredients in saucepan over medium heat. Bring to a boil, stirring constantly. As soon as syrup comes to a boil, remove from heat and pour, including the cinnamon stick, into sterilized 12-ounce bottle. Cap tightly and refrigerate.

GRAPE SYRUP

Utensils needed: Heavy saucepan
Cooking time: About 10 *minutes*
Quantity: 1 12-*ounce bottle*
Storing: Airtight container, refrigerated, up to 6 *weeks*

1 *cup grape juice*
2 *cups sugar*
1 *tablespoon lemon juice*

Combine grape juice and sugar in saucepan. Bring to a boil over medium heat, stirring constantly.

As soon as juice boils, remove from heat and skim off foam with a metal spoon. Stir in lemon juice.

Pour into sterilized 12-ounce bottle. Cap tightly and refrigerate.

ORANGE SYRUP

Utensils needed: Heavy saucepan
Cooking time: About 10 *minutes*
Quantity: 1 12-*ounce bottle*
Storing: Airtight container, refrigerated, up to 6 *weeks*

1 *cup orange juice*
2 *cups sugar*
2 *tablespoons lemon juice*

Combine orange juice and sugar in saucepan. Bring to a boil over medium heat, stirring constantly.

As soon as juice boils, remove from heat and skim off foam with a metal spoon. Stir in lemon juice.

Pour into sterilized 12-ounce bottle. Cap tightly and refrigerate.

STRAWBERRY OR RASPBERRY SYRUP

Utensils needed: Heavy saucepan
Cooking time: About 15 *minutes*
Quantity: 1 12-*ounce bottle*
Storing: Airtight container, refrigerated, up to 6 *weeks*

1 10-*ounce package frozen strawberries or raspberries*
2 *cups sugar*
½ *cup water*

Combine berries, sugar and water in saucepan. Bring to a boil, over medium heat, stirring constantly.

As soon as mixture comes to a boil, remove from heat and skim off foam with a metal spoon.

Pour into sterilized 12-ounce bottle. Cap tightly and refrigerate.

Sauces

CHOCOLATE SAUCE

Utensils needed: Heavy saucepan
Cooking time: About 12 minutes
Quantity: About 4 4-ounce jars
Storing: Airtight containers, refrigerated, up to 3 weeks

½ *cup cocoa*
2 *cups milk*
⅔ *cup sugar*
1 *teaspoon cornstarch*
1 *tablespoon unsalted butter*
1 *teaspoon vanilla*

Place the cocoa and half the milk in saucepan. Stir to blend. Add the sugar, cornstarch and remaining milk.

Cook over medium heat, stirring constantly, until mixture is thick and smooth. Remove from heat. Add butter and vanilla. Beat for about 2 minutes.

Pour into jars, cover and refrigerate.

This sauce must be reheated for serving.

NOTE: For variety, you may add to the above ½ cup crushed peppermint-stick candy, ¾ cup chopped nuts, or any fruit or mint flavoring in place of the vanilla.

BITTERSWEET CHOCOLATE SAUCE

Utensils needed: Heavy saucepan
Cooking time: About 15 minutes
Quantity: About 4 4-ounce jars
Storing: Airtight containers, refrigerated, up to 2 weeks

1 12-*ounce package semisweet chocolate bits*
¾ *cup Italian or any other very strong coffee*
1 *pound unsalted butter, chilled and cut in slices*
1½ *teaspoons vanilla*

Place the chocolate bits and coffee in saucepan over moderate heat. Stir until chocolate is completely dissolved. Turn heat to low if chocolate starts to stick.

Remove from heat. Beat in the chilled butter, bit by bit, until you have used it all and it is completely absorbed. If mixture gets too cool to dissolve butter, return to heat—but do not stir in butter while mixture is on the heat. Stir in the vanilla.

Pour into jars, cover and refrigerate.

NOTE: This sauce may be used cold to frost a cake or warm on any dessert. It is very thick and rich.

CHOCOLATE NUT-BRITTLE SAUCE

Utensils needed: Double boiler
Cooking time: About 20 minutes
Quantity: About 4 4-ounce jars
Storing: Airtight containers, refrigerated, up to 1 month

1 *6-ounce package sweet chocolate*
2½ *cups crushed nut brittle*
1 *cup boiling water*
2 *tablespoons brandy*

Melt chocolate in top part of double boiler over very hot water. When melted, add the nut brittle and slowly stir in boiling water.

Place the top part of double boiler directly over medium heat and stir constantly until nut brittle has melted. Remove from heat and stir in brandy.

Cool and pour into jars; cover tightly and refrigerate.

HOT FUDGE SAUCE

Utensils needed: Heavy saucepan
Cooking time: About 15 minutes
Quantity: About 4 4-ounce jars
Storing: Airtight containers, refrigerated, up to 1 month

½ *cup cocoa*
1 *cup sugar*

1 *cup light corn syrup*
½ *cup light cream*
¼ *teaspoon salt*
3 *tablespoons butter*
1 *teaspoon vanilla*

Combine cocoa, sugar, syrup, cream, salt and butter in saucepan. Cook over medium heat, stirring constantly, until mixture comes to full rolling boil. Boil hard for 3 minutes, stirring occasionally.

Remove from heat and add vanilla.

Cool and pour into jars; cover and refrigerate.

MOCHA SAUCE

Utensils needed: Heavy saucepan
Cooking time: About 15 minutes
Quantity: About 4 4-ounce jars
Storing: Tightly covered, refrigerated, up to 2 weeks

⅓ *cup unsalted butter*
1¼ *cups chopped nutmeats*
1 *6-ounce package semisweet chocolate bits*
3 *tablespoons orange liqueur*
1 *teaspoon instant espresso coffee*

Place butter in saucepan over very low heat. Stir until melted. Add the nuts and continue stirring until nuts begin to brown. Gradually add the chocolate bits, stirring constantly until chocolate is melted.

Remove from heat. Stir in the orange liqueur and the coffee. Blend well.

Pour into jars, cover and store in refrigerator.

This must be reheated for serving.

CHOCOLATE-MINT SAUCE

Utensils needed: Double boiler
Cooking time: About 15 minutes
Quantity: About 2 4-ounce jars
Storing: Airtight containers, refrigerated, up to 1 month

20 large chocolate peppermint patties
8 tablespoons heavy cream

Melt patties in top part of double boiler over very hot water, stirring occasionally.

Remove from heat and stir in heavy cream. Beat briskly to blend well.

Cool. Pour into jars, cover and refrigerate.

This must be reheated for serving.

PEPPERMINT-MARSHMALLOW SAUCE

Utensils needed: Heavy saucepan
Candy thermometer
Cooking time: About 20 minutes
Quantity: About 5 4-ounce jars
Storing: Airtight containers, refrigerated, up to 3 weeks

1 cup granulated sugar
½ cup cold water
1½ cups miniature marshmallows
2 egg whites, stiffly beaten
½ teaspoon peppermint extract
food coloring (optional)

Place the sugar and water in saucepan over medium heat. Bring to a boil, stirring occasionally. Cook to 220 degrees on candy thermometer. Add miniature marshmallows.

Remove from heat. Stir until all marshmallows are melted.

Very gradually, pour marshmallow mixture over the stiffly beaten egg whites, beating vigorously as you go. Add flavoring and food coloring and stir to blend well.

Pour into jars. Cover tightly and place in the refrigerator.

This must be reheated for use.

PEACH SAUCE

Utensils needed: Mixing bowl
Heavy saucepan
Cooking time: About 25 minutes
Quantity: About 8 4-ounce jars
Storing: Airtight containers, refrigerated, up to 2 weeks. May be frozen

8 *medium-size fresh peaches*
1 *cup sugar*
1 *cup orange juice*
juice of 1 *lemon*
2 *teaspoons vanilla*

Peel, pit and crush peaches.

Combine fruit with sugar and orange juice in saucepan. Bring to a boil, stirring constantly, over high heat. Reduce heat to medium and simmer, uncovered, for about 15 minutes, or until sauce begins to thicken.

Remove from heat. Stir in lemon juice and vanilla.

Pour into jars, cover and refrigerate.

MELBA SAUCE

Utensils needed: Heavy saucepan
Cooking time: About 15 minutes
Quantity: About 4½ cups (9 4-ounce jars)
Storing: Sterilized, sealed jars—indefinitely; airtight containers, refrigerated, up to 1 month

2 10-*ounce packages frozen raspberries*
1 *cup currant jelly*
1 *cup granulated sugar*
½ *teaspoon grated lemon rind*
1 *teaspoon cornstarch dissolved in* 1 *tablespoon cold water*

Place raspberries (with juice), jelly and sugar in saucepan over medium heat. Bring to a boil. Add grated lemon rind and cornstarch dissolved in water. Continue cooking until mixture is thick and clear, about 15 minutes.

Pour either into hot, sterilized jars with self-sealing lids (as directed on pages 112 and 113) or into a covered storage container for refrigeration.

NOTE: This sauce is used for Peach Melba—peach halves, vanilla ice cream and Melba Sauce. It is also good on plain cake or pudding.

BUTTERSCOTCH SAUCE

Utensils needed: Heavy saucepan
Cooking time: About 20 *minutes*
Quantity: 4 *to* 5 4*-ounce jars*
Storing: Airtight containers, refrigerated, up to 3 *weeks*

1 *cup dark corn syrup*
½ *cup granulated sugar*
½ *cup tightly packed light-brown sugar*
¼ *teaspoon salt*
½ *cup light cream*
2 *tablespoons sweet butter*
1 *teaspoon vanilla*

Combine all ingredients except vanilla in saucepan. Bring to a full, rolling boil, stirring constantly, over medium heat. Boil 5 minutes, stirring occasionally.

Remove from heat and stir in vanilla.

Cool. Pour into jars, cover and refrigerate.

HARD SAUCE

Utensils needed: Electric mixer
No cooking
Quantity: About 4 4*-ounce jars*
Storing: Airtight containers, refrigerated, up to 3 *weeks*

½ *cup soft butter*
1 *cup confectioner's sugar*
¼ *cup tightly packed light-brown sugar*
2 *tablespoons brandy*

In small bowl of electric mixer, beat butter until light and fluffy. Add all remaining ingredients and continue beating until smooth and well blended.

Pour into jars, cover and refrigerate.

BUTTER-RUM SAUCE

Utensils needed: Heavy saucepan
Candy thermometer
Cooking time: About 30 *minutes*
Quantity: About 5 4-*ounce jars*
Storing: Airtight containers, refrigerated, up to 1 *month*

1½ *cups tightly packed light-brown sugar*
⅔ *cup light corn syrup*
⅔ *cup cold water*
¼ *cup sweet butter*
dash salt
¼ *cup rum*

Combine all ingredients except rum in saucepan. Bring to a boil over medium heat. Cook, stirring frequently, until mixture reaches 230 degrees on candy thermometer.

Remove from heat and cool. When sauce is cool, stir in rum.

Pour into jars, cover and refrigerate.

This must be reheated for use.

NOTE: This is an excellent sauce for plain cakes.

RUM-RAISIN SAUCE

Utensils needed: Heavy saucepan
*Cooking time: Raisins–*1 *hour; sauce–*10 *minutes*
Quantity: About 8 4-*ounce jars*
Storing: Airtight containers, refrigerated, up to 1 *month*

1 *cup seedless white raisins*
2 *cups boiling water*
1½ *cups granulated sugar*
2 *teaspoons cornstarch*
1 *teaspoon lemon juice*
1 *teaspoon grated lemon rind*
2 *tablespoons sweet butter*
½ *cup rum*
6 *chopped maraschino cherries*
¼ *cup chopped nutmeats*

Place the raisins and boiling water in saucepan over medium heat. Simmer gently for about 1 hour.

Sift the sugar and cornstarch into the simmering raisins. Blend well and continue simmering for 10 more minutes.

Remove from heat and stir in remaining ingredients.
Pour into jars, cover and refrigerate.
This sauce must be reheated for use.

NOTE: Rum-Raisin Sauce is good on almost any fruit dessert or on plain cake. It can also be used as a meat glaze.

SHERRY SAUCE

Utensils needed: Double boiler
Cooking time: About 25 minutes
Quantity: About 4 4-ounce jars
Storing: Airtight containers, refrigerated, up to 1 month

- ½ *cup granulated sugar*
- 1 *tablespoon cornstarch*
- 1¼ *cups cold water*
- ⅛ *teaspoon salt*
- ⅛ *teaspoon nutmeg*
- *grated rind of* 1 *lemon*
- 1 *tablespoon lemon juice*
- 1 *teaspoon sweet butter*
- ⅓ *cup sherry wine*

Combine sugar, cornstarch and water in top part of double boiler over very hot water. Stir until sugar begins to dissolve. Add salt, nutmeg, lemon rind and juice. Place over medium heat and cook, stirring constantly, until mixture is thick and smooth, about 15 minutes. Lower heat and continue cooking for 10 more minutes.

Remove from heat and add the butter and wine. Stir for about 2 minutes to blend well.

Pour into jars, cover and refrigerate.

This sauce must be reheated for use.

Flavors

FLAVORED SUGARS

NOTE: These sugars can be used on toast or plain cakes or sprinkled on the tops of unbaked plain cookies. They are also delicious flavorings for tea, coffee, cocoa or punches. Vanilla Sugar can also be used as the basis for a cake frosting.

Utensils needed: Mixing bowl
No cooking
Quantity: Each recipe yields 1 *cup except Vanilla Sugar, which yields* 4 *cups*
Storing: Airtight container, in cool place, indefinitely

ANISE SUGAR

1 *cup sugar* — 1 *tablespoon anise seed*

Grind or pound anise seed and add to sugar, mixing well.

CINNAMON SUGAR

1 *cup sugar* — 1 *tablespoon ground cinnamon*

Combine sugar and cinnamon and blend well.

LEMON SUGAR

1 *cup sugar* — *grated rind from* 6 *large lemons*

Combine sugar and lemon rind and blend well.

ORANGE SUGAR

1 *cup sugar* — *grated rind from* 4 *large oranges*

Combine sugar and orange rind and blend well.

TANGERINE SUGAR

1 *cup sugar* — *grated rind from* 6 *tangerines*

Combine sugar and tangerine rind and blend well.

VANILLA SUGAR

(*Makes* 4 *cups*)

4 *cups confectioner's sugar* — 3 *vanilla beans*

Cut vanilla beans in half and combine with sugar.

NOTE: This may also be made with granulated sugar.

SPICED SUGAR

Utensils needed: Mixing bowl
No cooking
Quantity: About 1 *cup*
Storing: Airtight container, in cool place, indefinitely

1 *cup granulated sugar*
1½ *teaspoons cinnamon*
½ *teaspoon nutmeg*
¼ *teaspoon ground cloves*
¼ *teaspoon allspice*

Combine all ingredients in small bowl and toss with fork or spoon to blend thoroughly.

Pour into storage container, cover tightly and store in a cool place.

NOTE: Spiced Sugar is used in hot or cold tea, coffee or chocolate. It may also be sprinkled on plain cakes, ice cream or fruit.

FLAVORED COCONUT

Utensils needed: Mixing bowl
No cooking
Quantity: Each recipe yields 1 *cup*
Storing: Airtight container, in cool place, indefinitely

GRENADINE COCONUT

1 *cup flaked coconut* — 2 *tablespoons grenadine*

Toss coconut and grenadine lightly with fork to blend.

ALMOND COCONUT

1 *cup flaked coconut* — 2 *teaspoons almond extract*

Toss coconut and almond extract with fork to blend.

CRÈME DE CACAO OR CRÈME DE MENTHE COCONUT

1 *cup flaked coconut* — 2 *tablespoons crème de cacao or crème de menthe*

Toss coconut and liqueur with fork to blend.

NOTE: These are good cake or ice cream toppings. Flavored coconut is also a great addition to a fruit salad.

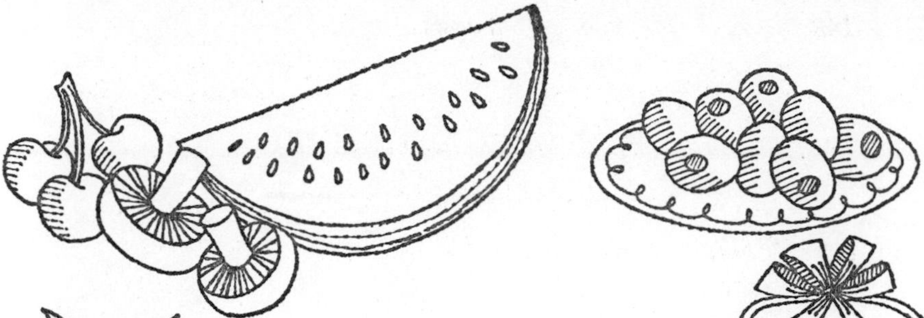

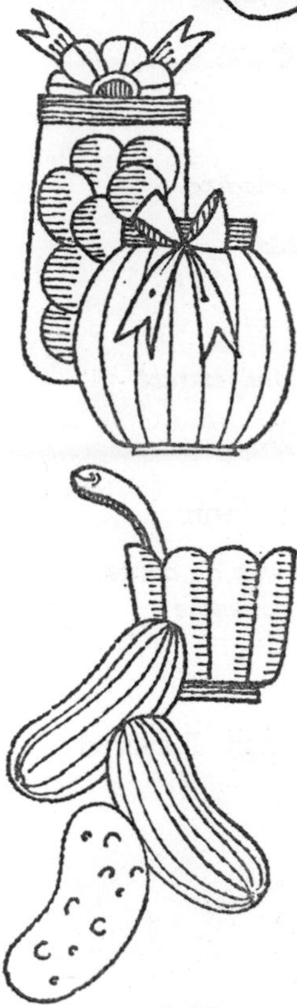

PART THREE

SOURS

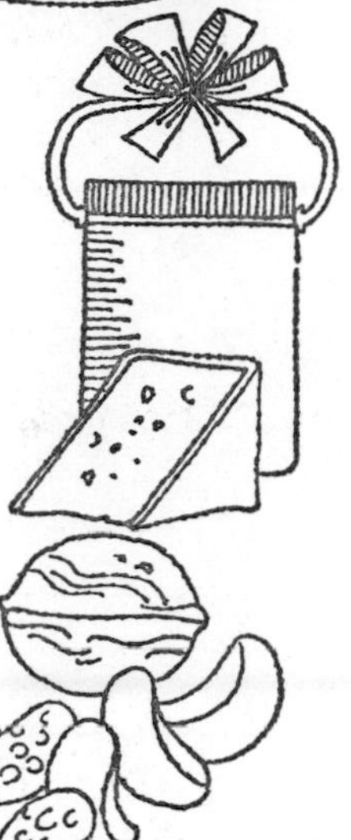

8 · Spiced Fruits and Chutneys

HOMEMADE spiced fruits and chutneys make excellent gifts, and the recipes included here are all quite easy.

Most of our recipes call for pint or half-pint jars. See Chapter 6 for sterilizing and sealing instructions.

When giving spiced fruits or chutneys as a gift, we recommend that you include serving hints. For instance, Spiced Peaches are excellent with roast duck, and Spiced Crab Apples go particularly well with ham or pork. Although a chutney is usually thought of as an accompaniment to a curried dish, it is splendid with almost any kind of roast meat or poultry. Chutney is a particularly good way to add excitement to leftover cold meats—for instance, Apple Chutney with cold ham.

For gift packaging, check Chapter 6 for ideas on decorating jars and lids.

Spiced Fruits

SPICED PEACHES

Utensils needed: Heavy roasting pan with lid
Preheat oven to: 300 *degrees*
Baking time: 2½ *hours*
Quantity: About 8 1-*quart jars*

9 *pounds medium-sized firm peaches*
4 *whole cloves per peach*
5 *pounds sugar*
1½ *cups cider vinegar*
3 *sticks cinnamon, broken*
1 *teaspoon ground allspice*

Dip peaches in scalding-hot water for a few seconds. Slip off skins while hot. Stick 4 cloves in each peeled peach and place in large roaster.

Mix sugar, vinegar, cinnamon sticks and allspice in a bowl. Blend well and pour over the peaches. Cover with lid.

Place roaster in preheated oven. Cook peaches for 2½ hours without disturbing. Turn off heat; let peaches cool in roaster in oven.

When cool, pack cold in hot, sterilized jars. Fill with syrup to about ½ inch from top. Seal at once.

SPICED CRAB APPLES

Utensils needed: Heavy kettle
Cheesecloth bag
Cooking time: 10 *minutes per jar*
Quantity: About 5 1-*pint jars*

4 *quarts crab apples* (6 *to* 7 *pounds*)
3 *whole cloves per apple*
8 *cups sugar*
1 *quart cider vinegar*
1 *quart cold water*
½ *cup red-hot cinnamon candies*
3 *sticks cinnamon, broken*
1 *tablespoon whole allspice*
¼ *teaspoon ground ginger*

Wash crab apples; leave stems on. (You may also use cooking apples, washed, cored and quartered.) Stick three whole cloves in each apple. Set aside.

Place the sugar, vinegar, water, red-hot candies and spices (tied in a cheesecloth bag) in kettle over medium heat. Bring to a boil. Boil, without stirring, for 15 minutes.

Put enough crab apples to fill one jar into the boiling syrup. Simmer for 10 minutes. Lift apples out of syrup with slotted spoon, fill jar and put on lid to keep apples hot. Continue this process until all jars are full.

Again, bring syrup to a boil. Pour boiling syrup through a strainer over apples to about ½ inch from top of each jar. Seal each immediately with self-sealing lid. Cool before storing.

PRESERVED ORANGES

Utensils needed: Covered casserole
Preheat oven to: 350 *degrees*
Baking time: 1 *hour*
Quantity: 4 1-*pint jars*

6 *firm seedless oranges free of blemishes*
water
¾ *cup light corn syrup*
2 *cups sugar*

Halve or quarter oranges. Simmer in water to cover for 20 minutes or until soft. Cool in cooking water.

Pour off cooking water, measure and add more water if necessary to make 2 cups. Mix with corn syrup and sugar. Boil for 5 minutes.

Put oranges into casserole and pour syrup over top. Cover and bake in preheated oven for 1 hour.

Pack oranges into hot, sterilized jars and pour syrup over top. Seal at once.

JUBILEE PEARS

Utensils needed: Saucepan
Covered storage container
Preparation time: Allow 2 *days*
Quantity: 2 4-*ounce jars*

1 1-*pound*-13-*ounce can pear halves*
⅓ *cup currant jelly*
1 *stick cinnamon*
⅓ *cup burgundy wine*

Drain pears, reserving 1½ cups of the pear syrup, and set them aside.

Put the 1½ cups pear syrup, currant jelly and cinnamon stick in saucepan over medium heat. Cook, stirring constantly, until jelly melts. Remove from heat and stir in wine. [*cont.*]

Place the drained pears in a storage container. Pour the wine syrup over them, cover tightly, and let stand overnight.

Pour pears into hot, sterilized jars and seal at once.

SPICED ORANGE PEEL

Utensils needed: Large glass bowl
Heavy kettle
Preparation time: Allow 2 days
Quantity: About 3 4-ounce jars

4 *cups sliced orange peel (from about* 10 *large clear-skinned oranges)*
1¾ *cups sugar*
⅓ *cup cider vinegar*
1 *tablespoon whole cloves*
3 *sticks cinnamon*

To prepare orange peel: Wash and dry oranges. Use a small paring knife to peel skin and a small amount of the white pith from the oranges in strips approximately 2½ inches × ½ inch. Measure peel and put into a large glass bowl. Cover with cold water and place in the refrigerator overnight.

Drain the cold water from the peel. Transfer peel to kettle, cover with fresh water and bring to a boil, uncovered, over high heat. As soon as peel boils, remove from heat and drain. Repeat. Then cover with water a third time and bring to a boil, simmer 10 minutes or until tender. Drain and set aside.

Put sugar, vinegar, cloves and cinnamon in same kettle and simmer 5 minutes to form a thick syrup. Add drained peel and simmer 5 minutes more, stirring frequently. Pour into hot, sterilized jars and seal at once.

GALA SPICED FRUIT

Utensils needed: Heavy saucepan
Cooking time: About 30 minutes
Quantity: 4 4-ounce jars

1 1-*pound can peach halves*
1 1-*pound can pear halves*

1 1-pound can apricot halves
2 teaspoons whole cloves
1 stick cinnamon
⅔ cup tightly packed light-brown sugar
⅓ cup cider vinegar
2 tablespoons brandy
½ cup drained maraschino cherries

Drain syrups from the cans of fruit and combine in a saucepan. Add 1 teaspoon cloves and the cinnamon stick. Put syrup over high heat, uncovered, and bring to a boil. Boil rapidly until it is reduced to 1½ cups. Add sugar and vinegar and simmer 5 minutes more. Stir in brandy.

Stud the drained fruit with the remaining 1 teaspoon cloves. Add the fruit and cherries to the syrup and bring to a boil. Spoon at once into hot, sterilized jars and seal.

Chutneys

QUICK PEAR CHUTNEY

Utensils needed: Heavy saucepan
Cooking time: 30 *minutes*
Quantity: 6 4-*ounce jars*

1 1-pound-13-ounce can sliced pears
1 lemon, thinly sliced
½ cup raisins
¼ cup minced candied ginger
½ cup cider vinegar
½ cup tightly packed brown sugar
¼ teaspoon nutmeg
¼ teaspoon salt
½ teaspoon mustard seed
1 teaspoon cornstarch

Drain pears, reserving 1 tablespoon syrup, and dice into very small pieces. Set aside.

Combine lemon, raisins, ginger, brown sugar, vinegar, nutmeg, salt and mustard seed in saucepan, bring to a boil and simmer 25 minutes.

Blend cornstarch with 1 tablespoon pear syrup, add to mixture and cook over low heat, stirring until clear. Add diced pears and simmer 5 minutes more. Pour into hot, sterilized jars and seal at once.

APPLE CHUTNEY

Utensils needed: Heavy saucepan
Cooking time: About 25 *minutes*
Quantity: About 10 4-*ounce jars*

- 5 *cups apple slices*
- 2 *cups light-brown sugar*
- ½ *cup cider vinegar*
- 1 *cup slivered candied ginger*
- 1 *cup thinly sliced onion*
- 2 *cups seedless white raisins*
- 2 *teaspoons chili powder*
- 1 *teaspoon salt*
- 4 *teaspoons mustard seed*
- 1 *cup chopped walnuts*

Chop the apples and combine with the sugar, vinegar, ginger, onion, raisins, chili powder, salt and mustard seed. Bring to a boil and simmer about 30 minutes. Add walnuts. Pour into sterilized jars and seal at once.

PEACH OR NECTARINE CHUTNEY

Utensils needed: Heavy saucepan
Cooking time: 30 *minutes*
Quantity: About 5 4-*ounce jars*

- 3 *pounds ripe peaches* or *nectarines*
- ½ *cup vinegar*
- *juice of* 1 *lemon*
- 1 *cup raisins*
- ½ *small onion, chopped*
- ¼ *cup slivered preserved ginger*
- 1 *teaspoon allspice*
- ½ *teaspoon cinnamon*
- ½ *teaspoon ground cloves*
- ½ *teaspoon ground ginger*
- 1 *tablespoon salt*
- 1 *box powdered fruit pectin*
- 4½ *cups sugar*
- ¾ *cup firmly packed dark-brown sugar*

Slice peaches or nectarines in half, remove pits and dice. Measure 4 cups fruit into saucepan. Add all remaining ingredients except white and brown sugars.

Place over a high heat, uncovered, and stir until mixture comes to a hard boil. Immediately add both sugars, stirring constantly. Bring again to full, rolling boil over high heat and boil hard exactly 5 minutes, stirring constantly.

Remove from heat and stir, skimming off any foam, for 10 minutes. Ladle immediately into hot, sterilized jars and seal at once.

ONION CHUTNEY

Utensils needed: Glass bowl
No cooking
Quantity: About 4 *4-ounce jars*
Storing: Refrigerator, tightly covered, up to 3 *weeks*

2 *large yellow onions*
cold water
2 *teaspoons cumin seed*
salt to taste
4 *teaspoons chili powder*
dash Tabasco sauce
juice of 3 *large lemons*
½ *teaspoon grated lemon rind*

Peel onions. Slice extremely thin and put into glass bowl. Fill bowl with cold water, stir onions (or rub with fingers) to wash well, then drain. Do this at least 5 times, draining after each washing.

Put drained onions back into bowl and rub cumin seed through palms of hands onto them. Add salt, chili powder and Tabasco. Mix well with wooden spoon. Pour on lemon juice. Add grated rind and mix again. Pour into hot, sterilized jars. Seal with paraffin. (Do not let chutney come into contact with metal.)

Onion Chutney is exceptionally good with cold meats.

9 · Relishes and Pickles

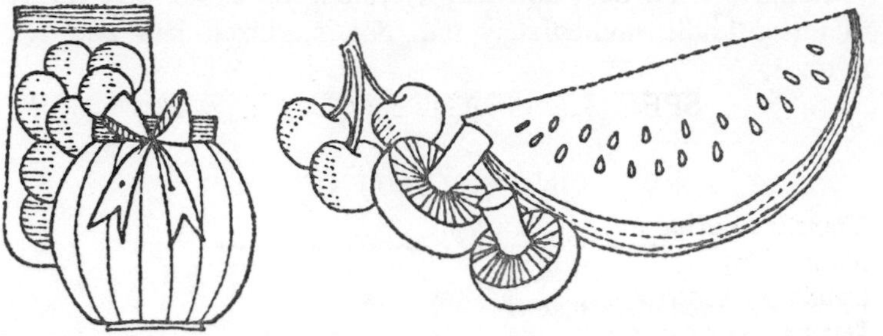

WE HAVE CHOSEN a sampling of the many different kinds of relishes and pickles that you can make. We have included fruit and vegetable relishes and pickles, using ingredients available throughout the year.

For large quantities of relishes and pickles, as well as for other recipes in this book, we suggest that you buy the produce from a farm stand out in the country rather than a local store. For the best results, you should use the very freshest vegetables that you can find. This is particularly true for cucumbers–if they are not fresh from the vine, they will not produce crisp pickles.

Most of the recipes call for standard pint or half-pint jars. We prefer jars with screw-on lids–either those saved from other foods or those specially made for preserving. Again, if you are purchasing them, we recommend the canning jar with the two-part lid.

For the best results in making the following recipes, you will need the same basic equipment that has been discussed in the introduction to Chapter 6. We also suggest that you have a pickling crock on hand, as some of the recipes call for one.

Relishes

SPECIAL CRANBERRY RELISH

Utensils needed: Food grinder
No cooking
Quantity: About 4 *cups*
Storing: Airtight containers, refrigerated, up to 2 *weeks. May be frozen*

1 *pound raw cranberries*
1 *large tart apple*
1 *large, firm winter pear*
1 *large juice orange*
1 *large lemon*
2½ *cups sugar*
1 *teaspoon ground ginger*
1 *teaspoon ground cinnamon*
½ *teaspoon ground cloves*
½ *cup chopped walnuts (optional)*

Wash all fruit well. Quarter and seed all except cranberries. Put through the medium blade of a food grinder. Do not lose juice.

Stir remaining ingredients into the chopped fruit. Mix well.

Place in covered jars or fancy containers. Store in refrigerator at least 24 hours before using.

CRANBERRY-PINEAPPLE RELISH

Utensils needed: Heavy saucepan
Cooking time: About 30 *minutes*
Quantity: 6 4-*ounce jars*

1 20-*ounce can crushed pineapple*
2 *cups sugar*
1 *pound cranberries*
2 *seedless oranges*
½ *cup seedless raisins*
½ *cup chopped candied ginger*
½ *cup toasted chopped almonds*

Drain crushed pineapple. Measure syrup and add enough water

to make 2 cups. Put liquid in saucepan, add sugar and bring to a boil, stirring until sugar is dissolved. Add cranberries and cook gently, uncovered, for 5 minutes.

Grate rind of 1 orange. Peel apart segments of both oranges and add them, with the rind, raisins and ginger, to cranberry mixture. Simmer, stirring frequently, for 20 minutes. Then add pineapple and cook 5 minutes more or until thick. Remove from heat and add nuts.

Pour into hot, sterilized jars and seal at once.

RAISIN RELISH

Utensils needed: Heavy saucepan
Cooking time: About 40 minutes
Quantity: 4 8-ounce jars

3 cups seedless raisins
2 cups packed brown sugar
water
4 tablespoons cornstarch
2 teaspoons grated lemon rind
½ cup fresh lemon juice
2 tablespoons finely chopped candied ginger
1 cup chopped nuts

In saucepan, combine raisins, sugar and 6 cups water. Bring to a boil, lower the flame and simmer, uncovered, 30 minutes or until liquid is absorbed.

Blend cornstarch and 4 tablespoons of water to make a smooth paste. Stir into raisin mixture, bring to a boil and cook, stirring frequently, 10 minutes.

Add lemon rind, juice, ginger and nuts. Reheat briefly.

Pour into sterilized jars and seal at once.

EASY RELISH

Utensils needed: Food grinder
No cooking
Quantity: About 4 cups
Storing: Airtight container, refrigerated, up to 10 days

6 large red apples
2 medium red onions
1 stalk celery
4 large dill pickles
½ cup cider vinegar
1 cup sugar
¼ teaspoon dry mustard

Wash, core and quarter the apples. Peel the onions and cut in half. Wash the celery.

Combine all of these with the pickles and put through the medium blade of a food grinder. This can be done directly into your storage container. Do not lose juice.

Add the vinegar, sugar and mustard to the ground mixture. Mix well.

Cover container and store in the refrigerator.

HEALTH RELISH

Utensils needed: Food grinder
Large mixing bowl
No cooking
Quantity: About 5 8-ounce jars

1 large head cabbage
4 medium-size onions
5 green peppers
4 red peppers
2 large carrots
2 cups sugar
1 teaspoon mustard seed
3 cups cider vinegar
1 teaspoon celery seed
¼ cup coarse salt
⅛ teaspoon cayenne pepper

Wash all vegetables; then peel, trim or seed them. Put them through medium blade of a food grinder and collect in mixing bowl. Squeeze out all juice and discard.

Add remaining ingredients to the ground vegetables and stir together until the sugar begins to dissolve.

Pack at once into hot, sterilized jars and seal.

CORN RELISH

Utensils needed: Large heavy kettle
Cooking time: About 40 *minutes*
Quantity: About 16 8-*ounce jars*

- 2 *quarts cut corn (about* 18 *to* 20 *ears)*
- 1 *quart chopped cabbage*
- 1 *cup chopped green pepper*
- 1 *cup chopped red pepper*
- 2 *large onions, chopped*
- 1 *quart cider vinegar*
- 1½ *cups sugar*
- 2 *tablespoons ground mustard*
- 1 *tablespoon mustard seed*
- 1¼ *tablespoons salt*
- ¼ *teaspoon cayenne pepper*
- 1 *teaspoon ground turmeric*
- 1 *cup water*

If corn is on cobs, boil for 5 minutes, dip in very cold water and cut from cob. Measure kernels.

Place all chopped vegetables and the corn in kettle and stir in all remaining ingredients. Place over medium heat, uncovered, and bring to a boil, stirring occasionally. Lower heat and simmer for 20 minutes.

Pack immediately into hot, sterilized jars and seal.

MOM'S PEPPER RELISH

Utensils needed: Food grinder
Large bowl
Cooking time: 30 *minutes*
Quantity: About 16 8-*ounce jars*

- 18 *sweet red peppers*
- 18 *green peppers*
- 4 *hot peppers*
- 16 *medium-size onions*
- *boiling water to cover*
- 2 *quarts cider vinegar*
- 4 *cups water*
- 5½ *cups sugar*
- 2 *tablespoons coarse salt*

Put the red and green peppers, hot peppers and onions through the medium blade of a food grinder. Collect them in a bowl and cover with boiling water. Let stand 5 minutes. Drain thoroughly.

Put the ground vegetables in kettle with 1 quart vinegar and 4 cups water. Bring to a boil, remove from heat and drain off all liquid.

Add the sugar, salt and additional 1 quart vinegar to the vegetable mixture. Cook over medium heat, uncovered, for 30 minutes, stirring occasionally.

Pack at once into hot, sterilized jars and seal.

CUCUMBER RELISH

Utensils needed: Food grinder
Large covered glass bowl
Heavy kettle
Preparation time: Allow 2 *days*
Quantity: About 16 8-*ounce jars*

12 *very large cucumbers*
4 *large sweet onions*
5 *tablespoons salt*
2 *cups sugar*
3 *quarts cider vinegar*
1 *cup water*
2 *teaspoons celery seed*
2 *teaspoons dry mustard*
3 *teaspoons cornstarch*
1 *teaspoon ground ginger*
2 *teaspoons turmeric*

Peel cucumbers and onions and put through medium blade of food grinder. Place in large bowl. Sprinkle with salt. Cover and let stand 24 hours.

Place the sugar, vinegar, water, celery seed, mustard, cornstarch, ginger and turmeric in kettle. Cook, stirring occasionally, until mixture comes to a boil.

Drain the cucumber mixture well. Add to the boiling vinegar mixture. Again, bring to a boil. Pack immediately into hot, sterilized jars and seal.

True Pickles

DILL PICKLES

Utensils needed: 1 sterilized quart jar with tight lid
No cooking
Quantity: 1 quart
Storing: Cool place

4 large stalks dill, very fresh
medium pickling cucumbers to fill quart jar
2 tablespoons coarse salt
1 tablespoon sugar
½ cup cider vinegar
water

Place 2 stalks dill in bottom of jar. Wash the cucumbers and pack them into the jar. Add the salt, sugar, vinegar and 2 more stalks dill to the jar. Fill jar to top with cold water. Seal at once.

Store in a cool place at least 6 weeks before using. Liquid may leak out of lid while the pickles are working. Do not disturb lid if this happens.

NOTE: This is an easy, crisp pickle, best made with cucumbers fresh from the garden. An easy morning's work will provide gift jars all year long.

LIBERTY PICKLES

Utensils needed: Large pickling crock or glass jar with lid
Large saucepan
Preparation time: Allow 2 weeks for complete process
Quantity: 2 gallons
Storing: Covered container in cool place

2 gallons pickling cucumbers, split
1 pound coarse salt
water
piece of alum the size of a walnut

2½ quarts cider vinegar
8 cups sugar
2 tablespoons celery seed
5 cups cinnamon sticks
large handful horseradish stalks

Pack split cucumbers into crock or jar.

Add salt to 1 gallon of water in a saucepan and heat to just below the boiling point. Pour salt water over the cucumbers. Cover and let stand 1 week.

Drain off salt water. Cover the pickles with unsalted boiling water and let stand 24 hours.

Drain off water. Cover pickles with boiling water in which a walnut-size piece of alum has been dissolved. Let stand 24 hours.

Drain off alum water. Heat the vinegar, sugar, celery seed, cinnamon and horseradish stalks together until quite hot but not boiling. Pour over pickles and let stand 24 hours.

For 4 successive mornings, drain off vinegar mixture, reheat it and pour back over pickles. On the fourth morning, cover pickles tightly and store in a cool place, to be used as needed. Let stand for about 1 week before beginning to use.

BREAD-AND-BUTTER PICKLES

Utensils needed: Large pickling crock or glass jar with lid
Heavy kettle
Preparation time: 2 days
Quantity: About 7 8-ounce jars

25 medium-size pickling cucumbers
1 cup coarse salt
water to cover
12 medium-size onions
4 green peppers
1 quart cider vinegar
2 cups sugar
2 teaspoons turmeric
2 teaspoons celery seed
2 teaspoons mustard seed

Wash the cucumbers. Slice very thin and place in crock. Sprinkle with 1 cup coarse salt and cover with cold water. Cover and let stand 24 hours.

Peel and slice the onions. Wash and slice the green peppers.

Add both to the salt water and cucumbers and let stand ½ hour. Drain and rinse in cold running water.

Place the drained vegetables and all remaining ingredients in kettle over medium heat. Cook, uncovered, stirring constantly, until mixture comes to a boil.

Remove from heat and immediately pack into hot, sterilized jars and seal.

MRS. PENCE'S PICKLES

Utensils needed: Large pickling crock
Heavy kettle
Cheesecloth bag
Preparation time: Allow 9 *days*
Quantity: About 18 8-*ounce jars*

8 *cups coarse salt plus* 8 *quarts water for brine*
3 *gallons medium-size pickling cucumbers*
5 *tablespoons alum*
boiling water
4 *quarts sugar*
4 *quarts cider vinegar*
1 *tablespoon allspice*
1 *tablespoon whole cloves*
1 *tablespoon mustard seed*
2 *cinnamon sticks, broken*

Make brine by boiling 8 cups coarse salt and 8 quarts water until salt is dissolved. Cool. Brine should be strong enough to float an egg. Test this by dropping an egg into it; if the egg falls to the bottom, add another cup of salt.

Scrub pickles. Place in crock and cover with brine. Let stand in a cool place for 1 week, then drain off brine.

Dissolve alum in 1 quart of boiling water. Cover the drained pickles with the alum water and about 2 additional gallons boiling water. Let stand in crock, covered, for 12 hours.

Drain off alum water. Cover drained pickles with more boiling water and let stand, uncovered, until water has cooled. Drain.

Place the sugar and vinegar in kettle. Tie the spices in a cheesecloth bag and add to the vinegar. Bring to a boil and continue boiling until mixture is slightly syrupy, about 15 minutes.

Place the pickles–left whole, quartered or sliced into chunks, as you prefer–in the boiling syrup. Bring to a boil again and cook until the pickles begin to look glassy, about 30 minutes. Do not overcook, as pickles should be crisp.

Pack into hot, sterilized jars and seal at once.

MUSTARD PICKLES

Utensils needed: Large pickling crock or glass jar with lid
Heavy kettle
Heavy saucepan
Preparation time: Allow 2 *days*
Quantity: About 12 8-*ounce jars*

1 *large fresh white cauliflower*
3 *dozen tiny pickling cucumbers*
1 *quart pickling cucumbers*
2 *dozen tiny white onions*
boiling water
½ *cup salt to each quart water*
2½ *quarts cider vinegar*
2½ *cups tightly packed brown sugar*
½ *cup flour*
6 *tablespoons dry mustard*
1 *tablespoon turmeric*

Wash the cauliflower and break into small flowerets. Wash the tiny cucumbers. Wash and cube the 1 quart pickling cucumbers. Peel the onions. Place the vegetables in pickling crock or jar. Cover with boiling water and ½ cup salt for each quart of water used. Cover and let stand 24 hours.

Put vegetables with the salt water into a heavy kettle and simmer, covered, until just tender, about 15 minutes. Do not boil or overcook. Drain off liquid.

Place the vinegar, brown sugar, flour, mustard and turmeric in saucepan over medium heat. Cook, uncovered, stirring constantly, until mixture is thick and smooth. Add the vegetables and cook until just warm throughout.

Immediately pack into hot, sterilized jars and seal. Let stand 2 weeks before use.

VARIATION: Instead of the cubed cucumbers, you may use 1 sliced red sweet pepper and 1 dozen tiny green tomatoes.

Vegetable and Fruit Pickles

PICKLED BEETS

Utensils needed: Heavy kettle
Cooking time: About 30 *minutes*
Quantity: About 4 8-*ounce jars*

5 *bunches washed raw beets or enough to make* 8 *cups sliced cooked beets*
2 *medium-size sweet onions*
3 *cups beet liquid*
1 *cup sugar*
2 *cups cider vinegar*
1 *dozen whole cloves*
18 *whole allspice*
1½ *teaspoons pickling spice per jar*

Cook whole beets until just tender, about 1 hour. Drain, reserving 3 cups of the cooking liquid. Peel and slice the beets and set aside.

Peel the onions. Slice thin and separate into rings. Set aside.

Place the beet liquid, sugar, vinegar, cloves and allspice in kettle over medium heat. Bring to a boil and add the sliced beets and onions. Again bring to a boil and boil for 5 minutes.

Place 1½ teaspoons pickling spice in the bottom of each hot, sterilized jar. Fill with beets and seal immediately.

PICKLED CARROT STICKS

Utensils needed: Saucepan
Preparation time: About 1 *hour*
Quantity: About 4 8-*ounce jars*

2 *pounds carrots*
1½ *teaspoons salt*
1 *quart water*
2 *cups cider vinegar*
4 *cups sugar*
1 *teaspoon mustard seed*
1 *tablespoon mixed pickling spice*

¼ teaspoon cracked black pepper
½ teaspoon coarse salt

Wash and peel carrots. Cut into thin strips. Place salt and 1 quart water in saucepan and add carrots. Simmer, covered, for about 8 minutes, or until almost tender. Drain, reserving 2 cups of cooking liquid.

Put vinegar, cooking liquid, sugar and spices in saucepan. Bring to a boil over high heat and boil gently until mixture begins to get syrupy, about 15 minutes. Add cooked carrots to the syrup. Simmer gently, uncovered, for about 20 minutes.

Immediately pack into hot, sterilized jars and seal. Let stand about 2 weeks before use.

PICKLED CAULIFLOWER

Utensils needed: Large glass container with cover
Large heavy kettle
Cheesecloth bag
Preparation time: 2 days
Quantity: About 8 8-ounce jars

4 *large fresh cauliflowers*
1 *large red pepper (optional)*
1 *cup coarse salt*
2 *cups sugar*
8 *cups cider vinegar*
1 *teaspoon mustard seed*
½ *teaspoon celery seed*
6 *whole white peppercorns*
⅛ *cup mixed pickling spice*
1 *tablespoon dried onion flakes*

Wash cauliflowers and break into flowerets. Dry well. Place in glass container. If you are using red pepper, wash and seed it, cut into thin strips and add to cauliflower. Sprinkle with 1 cup coarse salt. Cover and let stand for 24 hours in a cool place.

Place salted cauliflower under cold running water. Wash thoroughly. Dry.

Place sugar, vinegar and spices (tied in a cheesecloth bag) in kettle. Bring to a boil over medium heat. Boil gently, uncovered, for about 30 minutes. Add cauliflower (and pepper, if used). Bring to a boil and boil for 5 minutes.

Pack into sterilized jars and seal.

PICKLED MUSHROOMS

Utensils needed: Heavy saucepan with lid
Small saucepan
Small crock with lid or sterilized jars
Cooking time: About 20 *minutes*
Quantity: About 6 8-*ounce jars*
Storing: Refrigerated, tightly covered, up to 3 *months; sealed jars up to* 1 *year*

3 *pounds firm white mushrooms*
1 *cup red-wine vinegar*
½ *teaspoon coarse salt*
6 *cloves garlic, mashed*
4 *bay leaves*
2 *teaspoons grated onion*
1 *tablespoon white peppercorns*
¼ *cup olive oil*

Wash mushrooms. If large, cut in half; if small, leave whole. Place in saucepan with ½ cup vinegar and ½ teaspoon salt. Cover and simmer gently for exactly 12 minutes.

In a small saucepan, combine 3 mashed garlic cloves, bay leaves, onion and remaining ½ cup vinegar. Bring to a boil over medium heat and boil for 3 minutes. Add to the simmered mushrooms and cook for 5 more minutes or until just tender.

Drain mushroom mixture well. Place in crock or sterilized jars. Add remaining 3 mashed garlic cloves, peppercorns and olive oil. Cover and place in the refrigerator.

Allow mushrooms to age 2 days. Then pack in sterilized jars.

PICKLED GREEN BEANS

Utensils needed: Saucepan
Cooking time: About 20 *minutes*
Quantity: 3 4-*ounce jars*

2 *pounds fresh green beans*
salt
1 *cup vinegar*
¼ *cup water*
¼ *cup sugar*
½ *teaspoon hot pepper sauce*
2 *teaspoons dried dill weed*
2 *teaspoons mustard seed*
1 *teaspoon celery seed*

Wash and snap off ends of green beans. Simmer covered in boiling salted water until tender but still crisp.

Drain, cool and cut into ½-inch lengths. Cool thoroughly.

Mix vinegar, water, sugar, hot pepper sauce, dill weed, mustard seed and celery seed in saucepan. Bring to boil and simmer, uncovered, 5 minutes. Add beans and bring to boil.

Spoon immediately into hot, sterilized jars and seal at once.

GREEN-TOMATO PICKLES

Utensils needed: Sterilized canning jar with lid
Saucepan
Cooking time: Pickling solution: about 10 *minutes*
Quantity: 1 *quart*
Storing: Room temperature, covered but unsealed, 1 *week; sealed indefinitely*

Approximately 10 to 12 1½-*to-2-inch green tomatoes*
2 *bay leaves*
1 *teaspoon mixed pickling spice*
1 *large clove of garlic*
2 *small sweet red peppers*
dill (fresh preferred)

PICKLING SOLUTION:
4 *cups water*
2 *cups mild vinegar*
½ *cup salt*

Wash tomatoes, remove stems and drain. Pack tightly into jar. Fill empty spaces with some quartered tomatoes. Add spices and peppers to jar. Place a stalk of fresh dill on top.

Bring pickling solution to boil. Pour while hot into filled jar. Seal at once. See storing instructions above.

PICKLED CHERRIES

Utensils needed: Sterilized canning jar with lid
No cooking
Quantity: 1 *quart*

1 *quart firm ripe cherries, stems on*
1 *tablespoon sugar*
1 *tablespoon salt*
½ *cup cider vinegar*
water

Wash cherries well. Pack into sterilized quart jar. Add sugar, salt and vinegar. Fill jar to top with water. Seal at once.

Store at least 2 weeks before use.

NOTE: Use Pickled Cherries as you would olives or as a meat garnish or relish.

PICKLED PEACHES

Utensils needed: Large covered bowl
Heavy kettle
Cooking time: About 25 minutes
Quantity: About 6 quart jars

7 *pounds firm ripe peaches*
4 *pounds sugar*
1 *quart cider vinegar*
¼ *cup whole cloves, heads removed, tied in cheesecloth bag*

Dip peaches in scalding-hot water for a few seconds, then immediately slip off skins. Place peaches in bowl, cover and set aside.

Place bag of cloves in kettle with the sugar and vinegar. Bring to a boil over medium heat and boil for about 15 minutes, or until clear and syrupy.

Put enough peaches to fill one jar into the boiling syrup. Cook until just beginning to get tender, about 5 minutes; do not overcook.

Lift peaches out of syrup with a slotted spoon, put into sterilized jar and put on lid to keep peaches hot. Continue this process until all jars are full. Pour boiling-hot syrup over peaches to about ½ inch from top of each jar and seal immediately.

NOTE: Any extra syrup may be kept for use as a glaze for ham or poultry.

PICKLED WATERMELON RIND

Utensils needed: Pickling crock or large glass jar with lid
2 large, heavy kettles
Cheesecloth bag
Preparation time: 3 days
Quantity: About 5 8-ounce jars

½ large watermelon, or enough to make 2 quarts prepared rind
water
2 tablespoons salt
2 tablespoons alum
1 tablespoon crushed ginger root
1 tablespoon whole allspice
1 tablespoon whole cloves
3 sticks cinnamon, broken
2 cups sugar
1 cup cider vinegar
2 large lemons, sliced thin
4 cups sugar
3 cups cider vinegar

To prepare rind: Trim off the green outer skin and pink flesh from thick watermelon rind. Cut rind into chunks and place in pickling crock or large jar. Cover with 2 quarts water, salt and alum. Let stand 24 hours. Drain off alum water. Rinse well in running cold water.

Place drained rind in kettle. Cover with cold water and bring to a boil. Simmer gently, over medium heat, for 1 hour.

Tie spices in a cheesecloth bag and place in another kettle with 2 cups sugar, 1 cup vinegar and 1 quart cold water. Bring to a boil and boil for exactly 5 minutes. Remove from heat.

Drain boiled rind. Add rind and sliced lemons to the boiled syrup mixture. Place over medium heat and simmer for 30 minutes, stirring frequently. Remove from heat. Cover and let stand in a cool place for 24 hours.

Add 4 cups sugar and 3 cups vinegar to the rind and syrup. Place all in kettle over medium heat and bring to a boil. Boil gently until syrup is almost as thick as honey and the rind is translucent. If the syrup becomes too thick before the rind is clear, add about ½ cup boiling water as you need it.

Pack into hot, sterilized jars and seal immediately. Let stand at least 1 month before use.

10 · Savories and Snacks

THE TERM "Savories and Snacks" covers a variety of homemade gifts. It is a catchall of good things to add flavor and spice to ordinary ingredients–dips, spices, salad dressings and cocktail tidbits. Included here are flavored rices and nuts as well as cheeses and vinegars. People whose entertaining is most commonly a cocktail party are particularly receptive to these gifts.

Here is where your imagination with packaging can really run wild. Rices can be put into small, colorful drawstring bags. An assortment of cocktail snacks can be packaged together on a serving tray. Cheeses can be packed in small crocks or shaped into balls or rolled into logs. Dips can be given with cheeses and crackers or homemade bread. We like to combine several gifts and use them for a housewarming present. They are always happily received.

For decoration of jars, see the introduction to Chapter 6. You can use cottage-cheese containers wrapped in foil or decorated with colored tape. You can also purchase inexpensive containers at the dime store. Almost any packaging suggestion in this book can be applied to Savories and Snacks.

Nuts

FRENCH-FRIED ALMONDS

Utensils needed: Heavy iron frying pan
Frying time: 4 *to* 5 *minutes*
Quantity: 1 *pound*
Storing: Airtight container, in cool place, up to 6 *weeks*

¼ *pound butter*
2 *tablespoons olive oil*
1 *pound unblanched almonds*
seasoned salt to taste

Melt the butter and olive oil in frying pan over medium-high heat. When melted, turn heat to low and pour in the almonds. Cook, stirring frequently, about 4 minutes or until almonds begin to brown.

With a slotted spoon, remove almonds from butter. Drain on paper towel or a paper bag. When well drained, sprinkle with seasoned salt to taste. Cool before storing.

GARLIC ALMONDS

Preheat oven to: 325 *degrees*
Utensils needed: Shallow baking pan
Baking time: 20 *to* 25 *minutes*
Quantity: 4 *cups*
Storing: Airtight container, in cool place, up to 6 *weeks*

¼ *cup butter*
1 *teaspoon garlic salt*
¼ *teaspoon garlic powder*
4 *cups unblanched almonds*

Melt butter in baking pan in oven. Blend in seasonings. Add almonds and bake 20 to 25 minutes, stirring frequently. Drain on paper towels. Cool before storing.

CURRIED ALMONDS

Preheat oven to: 300 *degrees*
Utensils needed: Shallow baking pan
Baking time: 45 *minutes*
Quantity: 2 *cups*
Storing: Airtight container, in cool place, up to 6 *weeks*

2 *cups whole almonds, blanched*
¼ *cup butter*
2 *teaspoons seasoned salt*
1 *tablespoon curry powder*
salt to taste

Spread nuts in shallow baking pan. Bake at 300 degrees for 25 minutes, or until golden.

Melt butter in skillet and stir in seasoned salt and curry powder. Pour over nuts and continue roasting, stirring occasionally, about 20 minutes. Remove from oven and spread on paper towels to drain. Salt to taste. Cool before storing.

CHILI NUTS

Preheat oven to: 300 *degrees*
Utensils needed: Roasting pan
Baking time: 45 *minutes*
Quantity: 4 *cups*
Storing: Airtight container, in cool place, up to 6 *weeks*

2 *cups cashews*
2 *cups pecans*
¼ *cup butter*
2 *teaspoons chili powder*
¼ *teaspoon cayenne pepper*
½ *teaspoon garlic salt*

Spread nuts in roasting pan. Toast in preheated oven for 25 minutes, stirring occasionally.

Melt butter in skillet and add chili powder, cayenne and garlic salt. Pour over nuts and roast, stirring frequently, for 20 minutes. Drain on paper towels. Cool before storing.

DEVILED NUTS

Utensils needed: Heavy iron frying pan
Heavy paper bag
Cooking time: 3 *to* 5 *minutes*
Quantity: 1 *pound*
Storing: Airtight container, in cool place, up to 6 *weeks*

3 *tablespoons butter*
1 *pound cashews, almonds, pecans* or *hazelnuts* or *a mixture of all*
dash Worcestershire sauce
1½ *teaspoons salt*
⅛ *teaspoon paprika*
¼ *teaspoon cayenne pepper*
⅛ *teaspoon chili powder*
⅛ *teaspoon ground cumin*

Melt butter in frying pan over low heat. Add nuts. Fry, stirring constantly, for about 3 to 5 minutes, or until nuts are golden.

Remove from heat. Add a dash of Worcestershire sauce and stir to blend well.

Using a slotted spoon, remove nuts from butter. Drain on a paper towel. When well drained, pour into paper bag and sprinkle with spices. Shake well to coat nuts with spices. Cool before storing.

WHOLE ROASTED WALNUTS

Preheat oven to: 350 *degrees*
Utensils needed: Shallow baking pan
Baking time: 25 *minutes*
Quantity: As many pounds as you wish to prepare
Storing: Airtight container, in cool place, up to 6 *months*

Walnuts

Place unshelled walnuts in baking pan and bake at 350 degrees for exactly 25 minutes. Cool before storing.

NOTE: This is the simplest recipe we know. When roasted, walnuts have a superb toasty taste.

Appetizers

BEAN DIP

Utensils needed: Heavy earthenware bean pot
Preparation time: Allow 2 days
Quantity: About 2 quarts
Storing: Tightly covered container, refrigerated, 1 week. May be frozen

4 cups pinto beans
water to cover
2 cups chopped onions
3 cloves garlic, mashed
2 teaspoons ground cumin seed
6 tablespoons bacon fat
5 tablespoons chili powder
1 cup butter
½ pound sharp cheddar cheese, grated
3 drops Tabasco sauce
salt to taste

Wash beans thoroughly. Place in cooking pot and cover with water. Let soak overnight.

Add onions, garlic, cumin and bacon fat to beans and soaking water. Place over medium heat and bring to a boil. Lower heat and simmer, stirring frequently, three to four hours, until beans are very, very soft. If additional liquid is needed, add ½ cup boiling water at a time.

When beans are soft, add the chili powder and cook for about 5 minutes, stirring constantly. Using a potato masher or large wooden spoon, mash in the butter, cheese, Tabasco and salt. Blend until smooth.

Cover tightly, let cool, and store in cooking pot in refrigerator or in plastic freezer containers in the freezer.

This dip is to be served warm with corn chips, tacos or bread sticks.

CAPONATA

Utensils needed: Heavy frying pan
Cooking time: About 25 minutes
Quantity: About 4 pounds
Storing: Tightly covered container, refrigerated, up to 6 weeks

2 *pounds eggplant, cubed*
½ *cup olive oil*
4 *large tomatoes, peeled and chopped*
3 *large green peppers, chopped*
3 *large onions, chopped*
2 *cups pitted green olives*
½ *cup wine vinegar*
2 *tablespoons sugar*
½ *teaspoon oregano*
¼ *cup water*

Sauté eggplant cubes in olive oil over medium-high heat for about 15 minutes, stirring frequently. Add tomatoes, peppers, onions and olives. Cook for about 10 minutes. Remove from heat.

Mix together the vinegar, sugar, oregano and water. Stir to dissolve the sugar. Add to vegetable mixture.

Pour into covered storage container. Chill in the refrigerator at least 12 hours before using.

This is an excellent appetizer or can be used as a cold vegetable dish.

HOOMUS

Utensils needed: Food grinder
No cooking
Quantity: About 3 cups
Storing: Refrigerated, tightly covered, up to 1 week

3 1-*pound cans chick-peas*
1 1-*pound can tahina (ground sesame seed—available in imported-food shops)*
8 *cloves garlic*
juice of 6 lemons
salt to taste

Drain chick-peas, reserving liquid. Put the drained chick-peas, tahina and garlic through medium blade of food grinder. Add up to 1 cup reserved chick-pea liquid and juice of 6 lemons. Salt to taste and mix well.

Pack into decorative jars or crocks and store in the refrigerator.

NOTE: Hoomus may be given with Cuban Bread (page 46) or a traditional Middle Eastern bread.

MARINATED OLIVES

No cooking
Quantity: 1 *8-ounce jar*
Storing: Airtight container, refrigerated, up to 2 *months*

1 *8-ounce screw-top jar ripe or green olives with pits*
olive oil
red-wine vinegar
1 *clove garlic, crushed*
¼ *teaspoon cracked black pepper*

Drain all juice from olives and discard, leaving olives in jar. Fill jar two-thirds full with olive oil. Fill to the top with wine vinegar. Add the crushed garlic and pepper. Screw on lid and shake vigorously to mix. Allow to blend in the refrigerator at least 2 days before use.

BRANDIED BLUE CHEESE

Utensils needed: Mixing bowl
Wire whisk
No cooking
Quantity: About 1 *pound, or* 4 *4-ounce jars*
Storing: Airtight container, refrigerated, up to 1 *month*

½ *pound soft blue cheese*
¼ *cup soft butter*
2 *tablespoons brandy*
¼ *cup chopped toasted almonds*

Combine blue cheese, butter and brandy in mixing bowl and

beat with wire whisk until smooth. Stir in almonds. Pack into a cheese crock or 4-ounce jars, seal with paraffin (see page 113) and refrigerate.

BRANDIED BLUE-CHEESE POT

Utensils needed: Mixing bowl
No cooking
Quantity: About 2 cups
Storing: Airtight container, refrigerated, up to 1 month

1 *cup crumbled blue cheese*
1 *6-ounce package cream cheese*
2 *tablespoons mayonnaise*
2 *tablespoons brandy*
1 *teaspoon caraway seed*
½ *teaspoon garlic salt*

Combine all ingredients. Mix, with a wooden spoon, until well blended and fairly smooth. Place in covered storage container in the refrigerator.

TANGY CHEESE POT

Utensils needed: Electric blender or mixer
Small crocks or jars with tight lids
No cooking
Quantity: About 3 cups
Storing: Airtight containers, refrigerated, up to 1 month

1 *pound grated cheddar cheese*
1 *teaspoon curry powder*
1 *teaspoon chopped chives*
½ *teaspoon Dijon mustard*
dash cayenne pepper
½ *teaspoon onion salt*
⅓ *cup sherry wine*
1 *tablespoon peanut oil*

For electric blender: Blend half of the cheese and all the remaining ingredients on medium speed until smooth. Add remaining cheese and blend until smooth. If too thick, add about ¼ cup more sherry.

For electric mixer: Place all ingredients in mixing bowl. Beat at medium speed until well blended. If mixture is lumpy, use a large wooden spoon to smooth.

Place in storage containers and store as directed.

MEAT OR POULTRY PASTRIES

For pastry recipe: See Jam Pastries in Chapter 3 (*page* 73).

MEAT OR POULTRY FILLING

Utensils needed: Heavy frying pan
Cooking time: About 15 *minutes*
Quantity: About 5 *dozen*

⅛ *pound butter*
2 *cups ground, cooked meat or poultry*
⅛ *cup grated onion*
⅛ *cup grated celery*
1 *teaspoon chopped parsley*
⅛ *teaspoon thyme* (*for meat*) or *tarragon* (*for poultry*)
salt to taste
cracked black pepper to taste

Melt butter in frying pan over low heat. Add all other ingredients and cook until onion and celery are soft and translucent—about 15 minutes. Do not overcook, as filling will become too dry.

Fill and bake as for Jam Pastries. These may be frozen and warmed slightly when ready to serve.

For Salads

FRUIT-SALAD DRESSING

Utensils needed: Electric blender or rotary beater
No cooking
Quantity: About 2 *cups*
Storing: Airtight container, refrigerated, up to 2 *weeks*

1 *cup orange juice*
2 *tablespoons lemon juice*

1 cup peanut oil
2 tablespoons honey
¼ teaspoon nutmeg
½ teaspoon salt

Combine all ingredients and blend for a few seconds at high speed in an electric blender, or beat with a rotary beater until well combined.

Pour into storage container, cover tightly, and refrigerate.

MOLLIE'S SPECIAL SALAD DRESSING

Utensils needed: Electric blender
No cooking
Quantity: About 2 cups
Storing: Airtight container, refrigerated, up to 2 weeks

1 *6-ounce can tomato paste*
6 *ounces red-wine vinegar*
6 *ounces salad oil*
1 *medium-size onion, coarsely chopped*
1 *egg*
pinch sugar
pinch salt
pinch pepper

Empty can of tomato paste into blender jar. Fill empty can with vinegar and add to tomato paste. Refill can with salad oil and add to the tomato paste and vinegar. Add onion and egg. Blend at high speed for about 10 seconds. Add the pinches of sugar, salt and pepper and whirl just to blend. Pour into storage container, cover tightly and refrigerate.

SALAD SEASONING

Utensils needed: Mixing bowl
No cooking
Quantity: About 3¼ cups
Storing: Airtight container, in cool place, up to 3 months

2 *cups finely grated Parmesan cheese*
2 *teaspoons coarse salt*
½ cup sesame seed
¼ cup poppy seed
1 *teaspoon monosodium glutamate*
2 *tablespoons celery seed*

½ teaspoon garlic salt
1 tablespoon dried onion flakes
2 tablespoons parsley flakes
½ teaspoon dried dill
1 teaspoon paprika
½ teaspoon cracked black pepper

Combine all ingredients in a mixing bowl and stir to blend well. Pour into storage container, cover tightly and store in a cool place.

NOTE: For gift giving, attach these directions:

Sprinkle 1 to 2 tablespoonfuls on salad greens, as a seasoning with a plain oil-and-vinegar dressing.

Salad Seasoning is also good in cream sauces and as a garnish on baked potatoes.

THREE VINEGARS

Quantity: 1 pint
Storing: Cool, dark place

GARLIC VINEGAR

1 pint vinegar
1 or 2 cloves garlic

Add garlic to vinegar and let stand 1 week. Remove garlic.

TARRAGON VINEGAR

1 pint vinegar
3 sprigs fresh tarragon

Combine vinegar and tarragon and let stand 3 weeks. Remove tarragon.

DILL VINEGAR

1 pint vinegar
3 sprigs fresh dill

Combine vinegar and dill and let stand 3 weeks. Remove dill.

HERBED CROUTONS

Preheat oven to: 400 *degrees*
Utensils needed: Shallow baking pan
Baking time: About 7 *minutes*
Quantity: About 4 *cups*
Storing: Airtight container, in cool place, up to 1 *month*

½ *cup margarine*
1 *tablespoon olive oil*
1 *teaspoon crushed marjoram*
1 *teaspoon onion salt*
½ *teaspoon crushed chervil*
¼ *teaspoon crushed thyme*
1 *teaspoon crushed dried parsley*
4 *cups toasted dried bread cubes*

Melt margarine and olive oil in baking pan in oven. Remove from oven and add spices and bread cubes; stir until well coated with melted oil.

Return to oven and bake for about 5 minutes, watching to see that croutons do not burn. As soon as they take on a medium-brown color, remove from heat. Cool on paper towel.

Place in storage container, cover and store in a cool place. These may also be stored in plastic bags.

NOTE: Herbed Croutons are excellent in soups as well as salads.

Seasonings

CURRY POWDER

Preheat oven to: 250 *degrees*
Utensils needed: Flat baking dish or cookie sheet
Electric blender
Baking time: 15 *minutes*
Quantity: About 1¼ *pounds*
Storing: Airtight container, in cool place, up to 6 *months*

1 *pound coriander*
½ *pound small cumin seed*

1 tablespoon ginger root
1 dried hot red pepper pod
1 tablespoon sweet cumin seed
1 tablespoon mustard seed
1 cinnamon stick, about 2 inches long
1 teaspoon whole cloves
2 cardamom seeds
8 black peppercorns

Place all ingredients on baking pan, spreading to cover bottom. Bake at 250 degrees for about 15 minutes, or until the spices are very hot. Remove from heat and immediately pour into blender container. Blend, while spices are still hot, for a few seconds at high speed.

Pack into jars with tight lids and store in a cool place.

NOTE: You may wish to accompany a gift of homemade curry powder with recipes for different curry dishes.

SEASONED SALT

Utensils needed: Mixing bowl
Quantity: About 1½ cups
Storing: Airtight container, in cool place, up to 6 months

1 cup coarse salt
1 teaspoon dried thyme
1½ teaspoons dried oregano
1½ teaspoons garlic powder
2 teaspoons paprika
1 teaspoon curry powder
2 teaspoons dry mustard
½ teaspoon onion powder
¼ teaspoon dill weed

Combine all ingredients in mixing bowl and stir to blend well. Pour into storage container, cover tightly and store in a cool place.

Flavored Rice

NOTE: Along with this gift, be sure to attach cooking directions. The cooking time of flavored rices remains unchanged from that given on whatever kind of rice you use.

BEEF RICE

Utensils needed: Mixing bowl
No cooking
Quantity: About 4 cups
Storing: Airtight containers, in cool place, up to 6 months

- 4 *cups uncooked rice*
- 4 *tablespoons powdered instant beef bouillon*
- 1 *teaspoon coarse salt*
- 2 *teaspoons dried thyme*
- 2 *teaspoons dried parsley*
- ¼ *teaspoon cracked black pepper*

Mix all ingredients together in mixing bowl. Divide equally into four containers—jars with lids or plastic bags. Seal airtight.

ONION RICE

Utensils needed: Mixing bowl
No cooking
Quantity: About 4 cups
Storing: Airtight containers, in cool place, up to 6 months

- 4 *cups uncooked rice*
- 2 *packages dried onion-soup mix*
- ½ *teaspoon garlic salt*
- ¼ *teaspoon celery seed*
- ½ *teaspoon coarse salt*
- 1 *teaspoon dried parsley*

Mix all ingredients together in mixing bowl. Divide equally into four containers—jars with lids or plastic bags. Seal airtight.

SPANISH RICE

Utensils needed: Mixing bowl
No cooking
Quantity: About 4 cups
Storing: Airtight containers, in cool place, up to 6 months

4 cups uncooked rice
½ teaspoon ground saffron
2 teaspoons dried parsley
2½ teaspoons salt
½ cup dried sweet red pepper flakes
1 tablespoon dried onion flakes
1½ teaspoons cracked black pepper

Mix all ingredients together in mixing bowl. Divide equally into four containers—jars with lids or plastic bags. Seal airtight.

CHICKEN OR LEMON RICE

Utensils needed: Mixing bowl
No cooking
Quantity: About 4 cups
Storing: Airtight containers, in cool place, up to 6 months

4 cups uncooked rice
4 tablespoons powdered instant chicken bouillon
1 teaspoon coarse salt
2 teaspoons dried tarragon
2 teaspoons dried chopped chives
¼ teaspoon ground white pepper

Mix all ingredients together in mixing bowl. Divide equally into four containers—jars with lids or plastic bags. Seal airtight.

For Lemon Rice, substitute 1½ tablespoons grated lemon rind, 2 teaspoons dried parsley, and ½ teaspoon cracked black pepper for the last 3 ingredients of Chicken Rice.

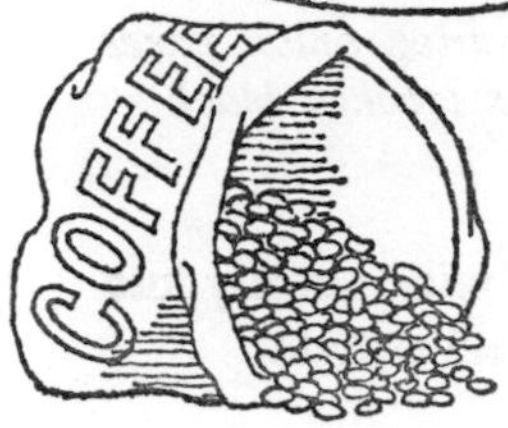

PART FOUR
DRINKS

11 · Festive Beverages

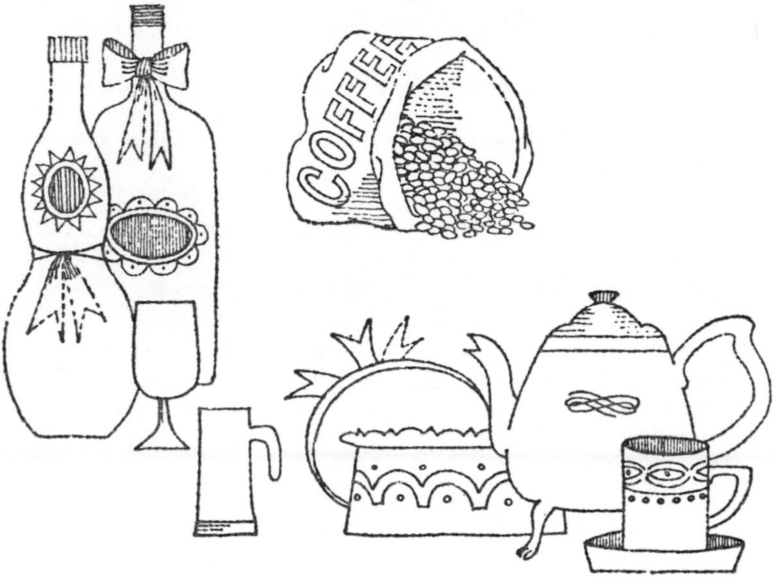

THE THREE BEVERAGES that we have included are very special ones. As gifts, they are superb given alone or may be accompanied by homemade extras: for instance, Spiced Tea with a Tea Bread; Mocha Coffee with any delicious cake; Coffee Liqueur with a tray of after-dinner tidbits.

The Spiced Tea is most attractive packaged in a small tea canister. It can, of course, also be packaged in plastic bags or tightly covered jars. Mocha Coffee is most easily packaged in the instant-coffee jar from which you have taken the coffee for the recipe. A bag of cinnamon sticks is a good addition to either of these.

Coffee Liqueur is best made and given in a clean (and odorless) half-gallon wine bottle. This type of bottle is usually so attractive that additional trim is not necessary, except perhaps a fancy bow tied around its neck.

Tea, Coffee and Liqueur

SPICED TEA

Utensils needed: Mixing bowl
No cooking
Quantity: About 2 cups
Storing: Airtight containers, in cool place, up to 6 months

½ *pound orange pekoe tea*
2 *tablespoons ground dried orange peel*
1 *tablespoon ground dried lemon peel*
2 *cinnamon sticks, crushed*
¼ *cup whole cloves*
1 *tablespoon chopped crystallized ginger*
1 *teaspoon grated nutmeg* (*or to taste*)

Combine all ingredients in mixing bowl and stir to blend well. Pour mixture into tea canisters or any other type of container with a tight lid.

MOCHA COFFEE

Utensils needed: Mixing bowl
No cooking
Quantity: 2 *2-ounce jars*
Storing: Airtight containers, in cool place, up to 6 months

2 *2-ounce jars instant-coffee powder*
½ *cup cocoa*
2 *teaspoons grated orange peel*
1 *teaspoon cinnamon*

Empty instant-coffee powder into mixing bowl and reserve the jars. At once add remaining ingredients and stir well to blend. Immediately spoon mixture back into coffee jars. The whole operation should be done as quickly as possible, as we feel that instant coffee begins to lose its flavor after it is opened. Seal airtight.

NOTE: With a gift package of Mocha Coffee, include the following directions:

Prepare as you would plain instant coffee or with ½ boiling water to ½ scalded milk. Add sugar to taste. Mocha Coffee may be served hot or cold. Either way it is delicious with whipped cream on top and a cinnamon stick as a garnish.

COFFEE LIQUEUR

Utensils needed: Heavy saucepan
Clean, odorless ½-gallon glass bottle with cap
Cooking time: About 10 *minutes*
Quantity: About ½ gallon
Storing: Airtight container, in cool place, up to 6 *months*

2 *cups boiling water*
3 *cups granulated sugar*
1 2-*ounce jar instant-coffee powder*
1 *fifth vodka or bourbon*
1 *large vanilla bean, cut into small pieces*

Combine 1 cup boiling water and the sugar in saucepan. Cook uncovered over medium heat, without stirring, for about 10 minutes to make a thin syrup.

Add 1 cup boiling water to the instant-coffee powder and stir to dissolve. Add the coffee to the syrup.

Remove from heat and cool to lukewarm. Stir in the vodka or bourbon and the vanilla bean. Pour into the clean ½-gallon bottle. Cap tightly.

Store at least 3 weeks before using. The longer Coffee Liqueur stands, the better it is.

APPENDIX

USEFUL INFORMATION

Packing for Shipping

No matter how tasty your homemade gift, if you pack it so poorly that it reaches its destination broken or spilled, no one will ever know what a good cook you are.

Breads and cakes should be wrapped in foil or plastic wrap, labeled and gift-wrapped. With the exception of fruitcakes, these should not be shipped long distances unless they are air-mailed on the day of baking. Wrap the gift-wrapped parcel in a thick layer of newspaper, place in a heavy box at least 1 inch larger all around, pack tightly with shredded paper and wrap with heavy brown paper. Mark PERISHABLE and HANDLE WITH CARE.

Some cookies are better shippers than others. Bar and drop cookies are among the best. We find that cookies arrive in better shape when they are wrapped individually and packed in the box in layers separated by crumpled tissue. Wrap the box in the same manner described for breads and cakes. Place the gift parcel in a heavy cardboard box at least 3 inches larger all around and proceed as above.

As mentioned in the candy chapter, we do not suggest sending candies long distances. If you do wish to try shipping candy, wrap each piece individually and proceed as for cookies.

Nuts are good shippers. Pack them in a can and place it in a box at least 1 inch larger all around. Pack the box tightly with crumpled newspaper so that the can is stationary. Label as with others.

All homemade gifts that are in bottles or jars must be packed very carefully for shipping. If you are shipping more than one jar in a box, be sure you allow ample room around each—at least 3 inches. Wrap each jar in a heavy layer of newspaper. Before putting jars in shipping container, cover the bottom with a heavy layer of newspaper followed by at least 1 inch of either shredded newspaper or shredded foam. (We highly recommend foam, as it will absorb more shock if the parcel is thrown about during shipment.) Place the wrapped jars in the box, well separated, and pack more shredded paper or foam as tightly as possible around them. Pack the top of the box just as you did the bottom, finishing with a thick layer of newspaper. Label as for others and add FRAGILE.

When shipping many different goodies in one large box, always wrap each in plastic or foil. If one thing breaks or spills, this protects others from absorbing the liquid or odors. Always label each item, so that the recipient will know just exactly what he has received.

Almost anything can be shipped if you take time in preparing the shipping carton. Go overboard on using newspaper, foam or tissue. It may add a little weight to the parcel, but your gifts will arrive intact.

Shopping Guide

H. ROTH & SON
1577 First Avenue
New York, N.Y. 10028

Spices, dried and glacéed fruits, kitchenware. Catalogue available.

MAID OF SCANDINAVIA
3245 Raleigh Avenue
Minneapolis, Minn. 55416

Unusual pots, pans and other kitchenware. Catalogue available.

MILES KIMBALL
41 West Eighth Avenue
Oshkosh, Wis. 54901

Unusual kitchenware and decorating trims. Catalogue available.

PAPRIKÁS WEISS
1546 Second Avenue
New York, N.Y. 10028

Spices, dried and glacéed fruits, special flours, kitchenware. Catalogue available.

HELEN GALLAGHER FOSTER
Department 802
Peoria, Ill. 61601

Unusual kitchenware and package trims. Catalogue available.